OTHER VOLUMES IN THIS SERIES

THE
BEST
AMERICAN
POETRY
2005

◊ ◊ ◊

Paul Muldoon, Editor

David Lehman, Series Editor

SCRIBNER POETRY
NEW YORK   LONDON   TORONTO   SYDNEY

SCRIBNER POETRY
1230 Avenue of the Americas
New York, NY 10020

SCRIBNER POETRY and design are trademarks
of Macmillan Library Reference USA, Inc., used under license
by Simon & Schuster, the publisher of this work.

For information about special discounts for bulk purchases,
please contact Simon & Schuster Special Sales:
1-800-6798 or business@simonandschuster.com

Text set in Bembo

Manufactured in the United States of America

1   3   5   7   9   10   8   6   4   2

Library of Congress Control Number: 2005049982

ISBN 978-1-4516-4647-4

CONTENTS

THE
BEST
AMERICAN
POETRY
2005

◇   ◇   ◇

David Lehman was born in New York City in 1948. He is the author of six books of poems, most recently *When a Woman Loves a Man* (Scribner, 2005). Among his nonfiction books are *The Last Avant-Garde: The Making of the New York School of Poets* (Anchor, 1999) and *The Perfect Murder* (Michigan, 2000). He edited *Great American Prose Poems: From Poe to the Present*, which appeared from Scribner in 2003. He teaches writing and literature in the graduate writing program of the New School in New York City and offers an undergraduate course each fall on "Great Poems" at New York University. He is completing a new edition of *The Oxford Book of American Poetry*, a one-volume comprehensive anthology of poems from Anne Bradstreet to the present. He initiated *The Best American Poetry* series in 1988 and received a Guggenheim Fellowship a year later. He lives in New York City and in Ithaca, New York.

FOREWORD

by David Lehman

◇　◇　◇

There are many reasons for the surge in prestige and popularity that American poetry has enjoyed, but surely some credit has to go to the initiatives of poets and other interested parties. Some of these projects involve a media event or program; just about all of them end in an anthology. Catherine Bowman had the idea of covering poetry for NPR's *All Things Considered*, and the book of poems culled from her radio reports, *Word of Mouth* (Vintage, 2003), makes a lively case for the art. The Favorite Poem Project launched by Robert Pinsky when he was U.S. Poet Laureate—in which ordinary citizens recite favorite poems for an archive and sometimes for a live TV audience—has generated two anthologies, most recently *An Invitation to Poetry* (edited by Pinsky, Maggie Dietz, and Rosemarie Ellis; W. W. Norton, 2004). Billy Collins, when he was Poet Laureate, campaigned to get the high school teachers of America to read a poem aloud each school day, and selected an academic year's worth for *Poetry 180* (Random House, 2003) and an equal amount for *180 More* (Random House, 2005). The success of the Poetry Daily website led Diane Boller, Don Selby, and Chryss Yost to organize *Poetry Daily* on the model of a calendar (Sourcebooks, 2003). The calendar is also a driving principle for Garrison Keillor, whose *Good Poems* (Penguin, 2003) collects poems he has read on his *Writer's Almanac* show, which airs on public radio five (in some areas seven) days a week.

The last several years have given us, in addition, high-quality anthologies organized around themes (*Isn't It Romantic*, eds. Aimee Kelley and Brett Fletcher Lauer; Verse Press, 2004); genres (*Blues Poems*, ed. Kevin Young; Everyman's Library, 2003), and historical periods (*Poets of the Civil War*, ed. J. D. McClatchy; Library of America, 2005). The number and variety of these (and yet other) anthologies make a double point about the poetry-reading public: it is larger than critics grant though smaller than many of us would like it to be; it reflects a period of eclectic taste rather than one dominated by an orthodoxy, as American poetry fifty years ago seemed dominated by the T. S. Eliot–inflected New Criticism.

As a rule, poetry anthologies receive even less critical attention than individual collections, but Keillor's *Good Poems* had a curious fate. Two reviews of the book appeared in the April 2004 issue of *Poetry*, the venerable Chicago-based magazine that inherited more than $100 million from pharmaceutical heiress Ruth Lilly in 2002. Both reviews were written by respected poets. NEA Chairman Dana Gioia wrote a courtly piece, employing a familiar book-reviewing strategy: begin with advance doubts (anticipation of "good poems, but probably not good enough"), acknowledge relief (pleasure in Keillor's "high spirits and determination to have fun, even when talking about poetry"), and progress to appreciation of the finished product. Gioia complimented the anthologist on "the intelligent inclusion of neglected writers" and praised Keillor for his *Writer's Almanac* show. Keillor "has probably done more to expand the audience of American poetry over the past ten years than all the learned journals of New England," Gioia wrote. He "has engaged a mass audience without either pretension or condescension."

When you turned the page to August Kleinzahler's critique of Keillor's anthology, your eyebrows had to go up. It was less a review than an attack on the Minnesota-based creator of public radio's long-running *Prairie Home Companion*, a weekly variety show with skits, songs, a monologue from the host, and occasionally poems from a visiting poet. Kleinzahler called the *Companion* "comfort food for the philistines, a contemporary, bittersweet equivalent to the *Lawrence Welk Show* of years past." That was gentle compared with his treatment of the "execrable" *Writer's Almanac*. Keillor has "appalling" taste, Kleinzahler wrote. Any good poems in *Good Poems* probably got there because a staffer slipped them in; a "superannuated former MFA from the Iowa Workshop would be my guess." (Though to my knowledge, there is no such thing as a "former MFA"—the degree is something you have for life and is not shed upon graduation—Kleinzahler's point was clear enough.) Keillor should be "burned," or perhaps merely locked up "in a Quonset hut" until he renounces his daily radio poem. In brief, Kleinzahler avoids the sound of Keillor's "treacly baritone" voice just as he avoids "sneezing, choking, rheumy-eyed passengers" on the streetcars of San Francisco.

When he gets around to talking about *Good Poems*, Kleinzahler articulates the anti-populist argument that underscores his contempt for Keillor. In every age, Kleinzahler says, there are "very, very few" poets whose work "will matter down the road." The effort to spread the word and enlarge the audience for poetry—an effort that Keillor enthu-siastically participates in—is a bad thing, because reading poetry often results in writing poetry, and most poetry is bad, and bad poetry is bad for you and bad for the art. Kleinzahler is vehement to the point of hyper-bole: "Poetry not only isn't *good* for you, *bad* poetry has been shown to cause lymphomas." Keillor's brand of "boosterism" may sell books and spur more poets to write, but it amounts to a form of "merchandising" that is itself "the problem, not the solution."

The anti-populist argument has its attractions. Many of us love poetry as a high art and regard our commitment to it as a vocation. And high art has its hierarchies, its idea of greatness or genius as something that few possess. As a poet you are continually inventing yourself by eliminating some models and electing others, defining your idea of what constitutes "good" and "bad." And if your aesthetic commitment is extreme, or your revolt against a prevalent style is des-perate, you may come to regard bad poetry as almost a moral offense. This is one reason we need criticism: it can help us to understand those crucial terms, "good" and "bad," whose meaning seems almost always in flux.

But anti-populist arguments tend by their nature to be defeatist and somewhat self-fulfilling. The dubious assumption is that if, against great odds, a poet or a poem wins some public acceptance, it must be bad to the precise degree that it has become popular, and not merely bad but contagious. Yet Gresham's Law—the economic doctrine that says that bad money shall drive out good—does not really apply here. No one hated bad poetry more genuinely and with greater feeling than Kenneth Koch. But as a teacher of children and nursing home resi-dents, and as the author of a genial "Art of Poetry," he suspended the natural arrogance of the avant-garde artist. Poems, he says, are "esthetecologically harmless and psychodegradable / And never would they choke the spirits of the world. For a poem only affects us / And 'exists,' really, if it is worth it, and there can't be too many of those." It may turn out that the enlargement of poetry's community of readers depends on a toleration not of bad poems but of other people's ideas of what constitutes a good poem. Moreover, if few poets in any given era will achieve the fame of a Keats or Whitman, it does not follow that the appreciation of poetry—great, good, and otherwise—is an activity for only a chosen few. Nor does it follow that the several originals among us are, in Kleinzahler's words, "drowning in the waste products spew-ing from graduate writing programs." Kleinzahler feels that the great talent of the nineteenth century went into the novel and that poetry's competition today is even stiffer and more diverse. He names "movies, television, MTV, advertising, rock 'n' roll, and the Internet." I don't buy it. The amazing thing is that despite all discouragement, significant numbers of brilliant young people today are drawn to poetry. Many are willing to make pecuniary sacrifices in support of their literary habit; more each year enroll in the degree-granting writing programs at which Kleinzahler sneers. Consider the growth of low-residency programs, in which faculty and students convene for ten days twice a year and do the rest of the work by correspondence. In 1994 when the Bennington Writing Workshop began, it was the fourth such program in the country; today there are more than two dozen. Sure, there are those who associate the rise of the creative writing workshop with the fall of civilization, but it remains a pedagogic structure of unusual popularity, and a talented instructor will know how to use its conventions to promote literary knowledge, judgment, and skill. As for Kleinzahler's contention that "American poetry is now an international joke," I think rather the opposite is true. But then he offers no evidence to support his position, while the evidence I could present to support mine— books published, copies sold, translations made, international conferences devoted to American poetry—Kleinzahler might dismiss out of hand.

The surplus contempt in Kleinzahler's piece—the anger so out of proportion with what had nominally occasioned it, and in such sharp contrast to the mild-mannered article that preceded it—generated a lasting wonder. It was as if one of the two reviews of *Good Poems* was in favor of civilization and the other in favor of its discontents; as if one spoke with the adjudicating voice of the ego, while the other let loose with the rebellious rant of the id. That the two pieces when juxtaposed failed to produce any ground for good-faith discussion seemed perfectly in accordance with the corrosive level of political discourse in 2004. "We campaign in poetry but govern in prose," former New York governor Mario Cuomo has said. But there was no poetry in last year's campaign rhetoric. I noted also that *Good Poems*, the modest and inoffensive title Keillor had chosen for his anthology, had not proved any more resistant to hostile comment than an anthology whose title dares to make greater claims for its contents.

The idea of running two reviews of the same book is one innovation that Christian Wiman has made since becoming editor of *Poetry*. There remains a problem with the criticism of poetry in America—too little of it is valuable—and Wiman is trying to do something about that. He is trying to create dialogue and exchange, and though not all attempts succeed, sometimes the failure is so spectacular that we're still talking about it months later. He seems to be discouraging easy pats on the back and encouraging people to go public with their peeves. And he prints letters arguing with the critics. All this has made *Poetry* a livelier, more compelling magazine than it had been. But it is also worrisome that the back of the book—the part devoted to criticism—has grown steadily. More voices, more pages, do not equal greater clarification. It is sometimes said with heavy tones of lamentation than in this day and age everyone's a poet. The criticism in *Poetry* implies that on the contrary everyone's a critic. And criticism is too often the sound of a gripe and the taste of sour grapes expressed with all the sensitivity and thoughtfulness of a midnight blogger.

Wiman spruced up the October 2004 issue by asking a band of poets to register their antagonisms and talk about them. In his editorial note Wiman says in passing that only the rare student will have the requisite "acuity and temerity" to challenge professors and anthologies by suggesting that "'Tintern Abbey' would be better without its last fifty lines." As Wiman notes, every editor has the right to be wrong, especially when the goal is to stimulate debate. But as one who cannot read "Tintern Abbey" aloud without tears at the end, and is all too familiar with college students' aversion to Wordsworth (though their own first-person-singular work may owe more to Wordsworth than to any of the other Romantic poets), I must rise to the defense of the poem as Wordsworth designed it. The last stanza, the poem's second climax, culminates in Wordsworth's moving prayer for his sister, Dorothy, as lovely a tribute in verse as ever brother penned for sister. But it is the passage just before the prayer itself—a single serpentine sentence spun out across sixteen lines of Miltonic blank verse—that is astonishing. It is like an equation in which either "nature" or "the mind," or the latter as a reflection of the former, triumphantly opposes evil and woe. The poet speaks

> Knowing that Nature never did betray
> The heart that loved her; 'tis her privilege
> Through all the years of this our life, to lead
> From joy to joy: for she can so inform
> The mind that is within us, so impress
> With quietness and beauty, and so feed

5

With lofty thoughts, that neither evil tongues,
Rash judgments, nor the sneers of selfish men,
Nor greetings where no kindness is, nor all
The dreary intercourse of daily life,
Shall e'er prevail against us, or disturb
Our cheerful faith, that all which we behold
Is full of blessings.

The passage is like a bridge across an abyss, with the reader progressing from joy across the chasm of low spite to a place of safety and blessing. It is a passage that you might quote for its smart use of line breaks. It expresses the "cheerful faith" that is the heart and soul of Romanticism—the conviction that the mind is superior to what it beholds and that imagination can redeem bitter experience. There then follows the "Therefore"—the prayer for Dorothy—that completes and unifies the poem, just as the address to the infant son completes and unifies Coleridge's "Frost at Midnight," the model for "Tintern Abbey." The "conversation poem" that Coleridge initiated and Wordsworth perfected has a form, and "Tintern Abbey" needs its last forty-nine lines to fulfill the demands of that form. Lop off the last stanza and you risk grave peril to the whole; as with the butchering of a cherry tree's branch, it could cause the death of the tree.

Defender that I am of "good poems" and advocate of great ones such as "Tintern Abbey" and "Frost at Midnight," I know it is up to readers present and readers future to decide whether *The Best American Poetry 2005* lives up to its name. Like its predecessors in a series now eighteen volumes strong, it reflects the best efforts of a guest editor, himself a distinguished poet, who went through the periodicals of 2004 looking for seventy-five poems that merit and reward our attention. Paul Muldoon, who made the selections, brings a unique transatlantic perspective to the task. Born in Belfast, an eminent figure in contemporary Irish and British poetry, Muldoon has lived in the United States since 1987 and is an American citizen. He holds a titled professorship at Princeton University, and when he began reading for this anthology, he had just completed a five-year stint as the Oxford Professor of Poetry, which is pretty much the highest academic appointment you can get in the United Kingdom. He had also recently won the 2003 Pulitzer Prize for *Moy Sand and Gravel.* I have admired his poetry since discovering *Why Brownlee Left* (1980) and *Quoof* (1983) when I worked on a *Newsweek* piece in 1986 about the extravagance of literary talent to have emerged in Northern Ireland, site of the "troubles." Muldoon's handling of a form like the sestina—"The Last Time I Saw Chris" in *The Best American Poetry 2004*, for example—or an ad hoc form like the errata slip ("For 'ludic' read 'lucid'"), his expert use of rhyme and off-rhyme, make his work exemplary. He is crafty, skillful, able to reconcile rival traditions, and I believe his take on American poetry will prove valuable for many years to come. Like Paul, I am proud of this year's book, and delighted to have had this chance to collaborate with him.

The late Thom Gunn observed that it may make sense to have movements and sects, with or without manifestos, when there is a "monolithic central tradition," as was true when Eliot and the New Critics ruled the roost. But when there is no central tradition, as now, the "divide and conquer" mentality—with poets "separating ourselves into armed camps"—seems less defensible. No volume in this series has been the exclusive province of a sect. While each editor will naturally represent most amply the poems he or she feels most in sympathy with, all have worked to transcend a narrow bias and labored to bring to the fore talents unlike their own. Lyn Hejinian, guest editor of *The Best American Poetry 2004*, when asked about the omission of certain redoubtable poets known to be her friends, said pointedly that she did not want to represent somebody with less than that person's best work.

Though poems may do no harm, the life of the poet is still felt to be full of perils. In April 2004, an article in the *Journal of Death Studies* reflecting a professor's study of 1,987 dead writers from different countries and different centuries revealed that poets tend to die younger than do other writers. Poets on average die at sixty-two, playwrights at sixty-three, novelists at sixty-six, and nonfiction writers at sixty-eight. This study in comparative lifespans came as news to CNN and the *New York Times*, which ran stories speculating on the psyche of poets. James Kaufman of the Learning Research Institute at California State University at San Bernardino, whose study caused the fuss, suggested that the poets' higher death rates might correspond to their higher rates of mental illness. Franz Wright, who learned earlier in the same month that he had won the 2004 Pulitzer Prize in poetry, was asked to comment on Professor Kaufman's study. "Since in the U.S., the worse you write the better your chances of survival, it stands to reason that poets would be the youngest to die," he said gloomily. Meanwhile, the backlash against National Poetry Month continues, as witness a brief item that ran in the satirical newspaper *The Onion* in late April 2005: "This month marks the 10th National Poetry Month, a campaign created in 1996 to raise public awareness of the growing problem of poetry. 'We must stop this scourge before more lives are exposed to poetry,' said Dr. John Nieman of the American Poetry Prevention Society at a Monday fundraising luncheon. 'It doesn't just affect women. Young people, particularly morose high-school and college students, are very susceptible to this terrible affliction. It is imperative that we eradicate poetry now, before more rainy afternoons are lost to it.' Nieman said some early signs of poetry infection include increased self-absorption and tea consumption."

Nevertheless, despite the glum news, more people are writing poetry, and going public with it. Rosie O'Donnell's blog features what she calls "the unedited rantings of a fat 43 year old menopausal ex–talk show host," mostly in verse. From a typically lively March 2005 entry: "marriot marquee / lois walks me in thru the kitchen—/ I felt like elvis presley—a head of state / a great fake important me." Who says poetry and Wall Street are incompatible? *Business Week* began a profile of Robert Smith, the fund manager of T. Rowe Price's Growth Stock mutual fund, with eight lines from Smith's "Up on Deck," which he says is a metaphor for risk-taking in the stock market. (The poem's risk-averse speaker "never saw how close the wreck / And never cheered the winds first still / As I might have up on deck.") Calvin Trillin gathered some of the politically charged doggerel he has written for *The Nation* and the book became a surprise best seller. "A lot of people in America hear the words 'rhyme' and 'poetry' and think it might as well be Canadian," Trillin quipped. He has no plans to give up what he calls his "deadline poetry." In "A Poem of Republican Populism" from *The Nation* of October 11, 2004, the Republican Party is the collective speaker. Here's the poem's conclusion: "Yes, though we always represent / The folks who sit in corporate boxes, / The gratifying paradox is—/ And this we love; it's just the neatest—/ The other party's called elitist."

News reports circulated that Saddam Hussein writes poetry in his airconditioned cell in a U.S. military prison. One poem concerned George Bush, though the leak did not specify whether it was number forty-one or forty-three. In the *New York Times* "men's fashion" supplement of September 19, 2004, Michael Bastian, the "man behind Bergdorf Goodman Men," held up Frank O'Hara as a fashion template. "We wanted to capture that whole tweedy, rumpled city-gun feeling, like a character in Cheever or Salinger, or like the poet Frank O'Hara," said Bastian, sporting a $995 Cantarelli tweed jacket and $390 Marc Jacobs chinos. Poetry is glamorous! For a reality check, we had the movie *We Don't Live Here Anymore*. Peter Krause ("Hank") plays a blocked writer, who looks sad despite getting word that *The New Yorker* has accepted one of his poems. Laura Dern ("Terri") tries to cheer him up. "You're getting published," she says. "It doesn't get much better than that." He replies sharply, "It's a poem, Terri. It's really nothing important."

One other celebrity almost made news as a closet poet last year. In March 2004, a senior editor at *Us Weekly* asked me to read and comment on a poem that Jennifer Lopez had written. The poem had three stanzas. The phrase "I am lovely" appears in two of the stanzas; in the first, the line reads, "I am lonely." Wanting to praise something in the poem prior to suggesting revisions or making criticisms, I singled out the progress from "lonely" to "lovely"—only to learn that the variation was the product of a typo in an editor's e-mail. In the end, the story didn't run, because more pressing news bumped it: Tom Cruise and Penelope Cruz had broken up. It remains a pleasure to welcome J.Lo to the poets' club, which is as democratic among the living as it is elitist when canons are fixed and all entrants are posthumous.

In View of the Fact

◇ ◇ ◇

The people of my time are passing away: my
wife is baking for a funeral, a 60-year-old who

died suddenly, when the phone rings, and it's
Ruth we care so much about in intensive care:

it was once weddings that came so thick and
fast, and then, first babies, such a hullabaloo:

now, it's this that and the other and somebody
else gone or on the brink: well, we never

thought we would live forever (although we did)
and now it looks like we won't: some of us

are losing a leg to diabetes, some don't know
what they went downstairs for, some know that

a hired watchful person is around, some like
to touch the cane tip into something steady,

so nice: we have already lost so many,
brushed the loss of ourselves ourselves: our

address books for so long a slow scramble now
are palimpsests, scribbles and scratches: our

index cards for Christmases, birthdays,
halloweens drop clean away into sympathies:

I Want to Be Your Shoebox

◇　◇　◇

Memphis Minnie's blues line "I want to be your chauffeur"
was miscopied in an early Folkways recording song tran-
scription as "I want to be your shoebox."

I want to be your shoebox
I want to be your Fort Knox
I want to be your equinox

I want to be your paradox
I want to be your pair of socks
I want to be your paradise

I want to be your pack of lies
I want to be your snake eyes
I want to be your Mac with fries

I want to be your moonlit estuary
I want to be your day missing in February
I want to be your floating dock dairy

I want to be your pocket handkerchief
I want to be your mischief
I want to be your slow pitch

I want to be your fable without a moral
Under a table of black elm I want to be your Indiana morel
Casserole. Your drum roll. Your trompe l'oeil

I want to be your biscuits
I want to be your business
I want to be your beeswax

I want to be your milk money
I want to be your Texas Apiary Honey
I want to be your Texas. Honey

I want to be your cheap hotel
I want to be your lipstick by Chanel
I want to be your secret passage

All written in Braille. I want to be
All the words you can't spell
I want to be your International

House of Pancakes. I want to be your reel after reel
Of rough takes. I want to be your Ouija board
I want to be your slum-lord. Hell

I want to be your made-to-order smorgasbord
I want to be your autobahn
I want to be your Audubon

I want to be your Chinese bug radical
I want to be your brand-new set of radials
I want to be your old time radio

I want to be your pro and your con
I want to be your Sunday morning ritual
(Demons be gone!) Your constitutional

Your habitual—
I want to be your Tinkertoy
Man, I want to be your best boy

I want to be your chauffeur
I want to be your chauf-
feur, your shofar, I want to be your go for

I liked the violence, the big shrieking,
And the jail time, and the thinking.

(Show off! Show off! Show off!)

from *POOL*

The Beats

◊   ◊   ◊

some keep trying to connect me with
the beats
but I was vastly unpublished in the
50's
and
I very much
disliked their vanity and
all that
public
postering.

and when I met most of them
later in my life
I still felt that most of my
feelings toward
them
were the
same.

some accepted
that; others thought that I
should change my
viewpoint.

my viewpoint remained the
same: writing is done
one person
at a time

one place
at a time

and all the gatherings
and tenderings of
proclamations toward the
flock
had very little
to do
with anything.

any one of those
could have made it as a
shoe salesman or a
used car
salesman

and they still
could
instead of bitching about
the changes of the fates and
the ways

even
still
now:

from the sad university
lecterns
these hucksters of the
despoiled word
working the
hand-outs
still talking that
dumb shit.

from *New York Quarterly*

Irregular Masks

◇　◇　◇

In relation to each other men are like irregular verbs
in different languages; nearly all the verbs are slightly irregular.
　　　　　　　　　　　　　　　　　　—Kierkegaard

They had beaten their heads against the walls of waves
　　　until a thousand green fish glittered to the surface

had drawn your inside thigh-blood, silent
　　　for a slow pint at the neighborhood pub

with their hair trailing behind them, had fled all bad
　　　words hung from the attic rafters overnight . . .

still those who, singing, had begun
　　　masturbating their way back to original sin, or

thousands, born to alcoholics, with sorrow as large as
　　　houseboats, have drunk the hand-wash of airport pickpockets

and others blindfolded by luck, caught the hurricane's eye
　　　to move in with the summer storm's shearing, for

another who has burst the helium balloon you bore in mind
　　　like a glow-in-the-dark apple the doctor gave away . . .

oh, how many more have broadcast, breakneck, their own
　　　breathing, told the moon it was the sleeper's open mouth

in the outskirts of the city, who have fallen to their knees
　　　　to see the shape of the world on the back of a baby's head

with those, serious, knowing real consequence
　　　　was a matter of verb tense's wear and tear on the past, that no two

faces are the same, just like any stunned Vermont snowflake father said,
　　　　disappearing easy as its memory, once it reached your skin.

from *The Los Angeles Review*

Seven Changs

◊   ◊   ◊

At night your growth rate doubles and each morning I spot
yet another Chang

in the newspaper, staring at me with its dull lamps. I limp up
a mountainside

toward a growing opal. Oracle, is this the way up to the little office
with orange lights?

Let's not argue this time. For the last time, we argued
over the arrival

of another Victoria Chang. Changed from Valerie to Victoria
and now my ruin,

for she, a track star, runs faster than a seashore. Shared bunks
were never favored by me,

a has-been-girl or even worse, a not-yet-girl. And don't even mention
the others—

faces smashed against the door, Helen Chang, Heather Chang,
Hilary Chang.

And with each new Chang, the shock of the world goes down,
drawn to the next eyeless eel

or the one-legged constellation. The next seven Victoria Changs,
all victorious,

in rows, each a little taller than the last. Their fevered footsteps persist,
fist me into midnights.

from *Michigan Quarerly Review*

To Jacques Pépin

◇   ◇   ◇

Touch me
with your impeccably clean hands.
Go ahead: Say *beutter*, instead of *butter*.
I can take it.

I love your rhapsodies of oil.
You are hypnotic as you pat
a chicken's rump with your right hand, swirl
your ruby glass in the left.

For a Frenchman,
you are remarkably open
to wines vinted by Californians.
Don't misunderstand.

I never intended any innuendo,
but I dream of being food in your kitchen.
Every night I become a perfect tomato,
a parcel of pastry, crimped and tender.

Give me away in a frock of parchment paper. Fold
me in. Slick me with a little clarified gold.

from *Gastronomica*

The Poets March on Washington

◇　◇　◇

What do we want?
Immortality!
When do we want it?
Now!

What do we want?
Immortality!
When do we want it?
Now!

What do we want?
Immorality!
When do we want it?
Now

from *Jacket*

Urban Myth

◇ ◇ ◇

A couple awaiting the arrival of their first-born delivers instead a ring-tailed lemur. They are beside themselves. The father beats the obstetrician with clenched fists. He curses the nurses and flings himself to the floor bawling. The mother stands up on the table and denounces God. The next day they go home. The lemur eats all of the houseplants and defecates in the sink. It refuses to come down from the refrigerator and keeps them up all night chasing flies along the window screens. The parents are mortified, but being optimistic people they remain patient. They dress the lemur as a boy and name it Colin. They send it to the finest schools and indulge it with every extravagance. Finally their hard work pays off. One morning upon entering the nursery they find a neat stack of money in the lemur's place.

from *Sentence*

Five Roses in the Morning

◇   ◇   ◇

March 16, 2003

On TV the showbiz of war,
so I turn it off
wishing I could turn it off,
and glance at the five white roses
in front of the mirror on the mantel,
looking like ten.
That they were purchased out of love
and are not bloody red
won't change a goddamned thing—
goddamned things, it seems, multiplying
every day. Last night
the roses numbered six, but she chose
to wear one in her hair,
and she was more beautiful
because she believed she was.
It changed the night a little.
For us, I mean.

from *The Iowa Review*

Everything I Needed to Know

◊   ◊   ◊

Ashes, Ashes, we fall on our asses
because the teacher has us. Rodeo
clowns make about as much sense, but then they
don't graduate from kindergarten
early either. Neither did they have
for their teacher Mrs. Cunningham, whose
grave countenance no kid had the word for:
Her is no bull sitter. Her is squeezing
in chair, knees together. Her is a locked
jaw with lips like a bad ventriloquist's.
Kind of like a lady Clutch Cargo. Or
like the bride of a Nordic Frankenstein,
motherless but blonde, beautiful, and big.
Nobody here knows she has another
occupation but me. I'm her little
Picasso, her baby ham, and cunning.
"Quit staring, Karl Curtis," she says, looking
right at me. She knows I know for a split
second she disappeared and does not want
to reveal her secret identity
underneath. I know she knows I draw some
very naked ideas. Later, when
we go around and tell in tones like the
xylophone's, girls always first, what it is
you want to be when you grow up, I say
Zorro because a poet needs a mask.

from *Beloit Poetry Journal* and *Poetry Daily*

The Revolution

◇　◇　◇

Remember it was early—we were still in the dark
slots of the narrow beds, the room twitching and burning
from all night TV—then voices—almost *lively*—

for this place, I think, unsheathing myself from the damp
  bedding to the cool and cluttered eight-story commotion—a burn
of sound, those voices, a Braille of noise.

I can't remember what broke the wash of listening,
what turned it (like a boat steered hard into its own wake) into sight:
  one or two floors below us, an answer to your question—

you are up and beside me now—*what is that?* was dragged by—
  window, wall, window, wall—locked in the arms of two men
and trying to bite her way out of their official embrace.

Did I mention—leaning out—now—to put ourselves into the courtyard
where a spill of images lengthened the view, we stared
  into the hall of our hotel, along which a woman

in a nightgown was dragged screaming
  like something metal opening against its will,
and their voices trailed behind to scuff out the marrings

her screaming broke open in the air.
We saw her, then she was disappeared by wall, we saw her
  naked feet skidding on the stone floor. Wind blew this way and that

in the immense eight-storied courtyard. And these two facts:
her gown was almost torn from her and that we stood staring—
what could be done—there had been trouble, we knew, betrayals.

Who was to say she was innocent.

from *Slate*

Pre-Raphaelite Pinups

◇   ◇   ◇

No one is saying how it came to be this way.
Sex is and is not part of the picture.

•

Too many people
wearing too many clothes,
thinking too few things.

•

The wallpaper is the real center of attention,
the figures mostly background music.

There is a rhythm to their eating.
One contemplates his wine,
another drinks it.

•

I never noticed it before,
but that angel's feet are on fire!

•

It's a penitent's head
they've pasted on a voluptuous body.

•

Why, she's practically an insect herself.

•

Look how many worlds are woven
with the silly-string of the Fates.

•

The wheat field was like a drive-in movie
for the shepherd and his date.

•

The berry-boy offers his handful of red
to the gray little girl.

It's all in the fold,
the fertility dance of being draped over . . .

•

One could panel a library
with the grain of her hair.

•

Can't you see I'm just a poor,
blind, accordion-playing lesbian?

Do not disturb the visionary butterfly
at work in me.

•

The heretic wears a pretty demonic
apron and crown,

while Medusa's blue hairnet
tangles even the trees.

•

A squirrel, a robin;
an army of innocence
waits to molest a young girl—
asleep and unaware.

•

But isn't every story an allegory—
every house strewn with alchemical symbols like these?

•

Ach—but that rainbow is loud!
Too much beauty makes a person faint.

from *The New Yorker*

The Magical Sadness
of Omar Cáceres

◇　◇　◇

A white road crosses its motionless storm,
vernal pool where frogs live trapped in archaic hail.
I've wasted too much moonlight
and sit gazing through the small hole in my dress at Monday's naked nail.

Manchuria, I feel your invasion!
Suddenly we are ourselves, without brushes, lawn-mowers, or bars.
I confess the crimes against my monsoon self—
these chess words, slippery with blood,
they are my pistons, my petrol, the fits of memory scrawled in a prison hulk log.
Cockroaches cross the deck   moving from Picasso to snowman.

The thought lost to the eyes of a unicorn reappears in a dog's bark.
Dressed in resistance, I laud the most important leader in the United States:
Mickey Mouse, legislator of urban alcohol adieu.
My courtesan instructs me in the wrecked balcony of her arms.
The idol? A chessboard of truffles and snow.
Unlike comrade Huidobro, I'm a whittled id,
a City Hall boss standing on the prison steps
thriving like a burnt-out sun,
a sun which never imagined a lamp.
O summation of Chile! A man loves only his obscure wife.

To run with the nectar, to bypass alarm.
Is not joy somehow canopic?
What moves in the air: ways that are not the way,

the whey of snow, way of the flayed flake.
My slash is yours, riptides amassing.
O Chilean summation! I poke into the moon's watery lace.
Between sequitur and non- falls the imagination.
"There is grandeur in this life, with its several powers."
Spare the gestures. Nothing for show.
I am neither aft nor fore, for foreafter,
nor ever to be aforementioned again.

I hear Neruda—he's a langoustine of a man,
a violet maiden in multicolored fleece,
both hands paralyzed from swatting political lice.
Neruda! A swiller of a gale, a snood disguised as a church,
rutabaga in cleats, something found on the beach which,
as you fondle it, urinates in your heart. Neruda,
what is truly to be found under his tray of forceps and sledges?

Passing mons Veneris clouds.
The translucence of human flesh.
Ceremonial lenses made of ice, brought down from Andean peaks.
A rainbow defective in a single hue.
Uteral squids relaxing in a bathroom sink.
The spider *Dolomedes urinator* which runs simultaneously in two worlds.
The sound of air in a cave.
Sensation of longing for an eclipse powerful enough to darken death.
Changes in the light initiated by a stranger's arrival.
—Chilean marvels, equal to the Surreal.

I prepared. Waited to be called.
Cut logs, laid a hearth. Burned my valentines.
Visited the Incan adoritories on Mount Llullaillaco.
Examined the grave goods of The Prince of Mount Plomo.
Which is to say: I prepared. Set the cauldron boiling,
spliced postcards from Isla Negra with photos of infants left out in the snow.
Mastered myself. Arrived in Harar with only 10 camels.
Sketched each waterfall. Took out no personal ads.
I faced fear, then clarity, then power.

Tonight I have a meeting with the last enemy of the man of knowledge.
In his uncorked left testicle, it has been raining for years.

from *Fence* and *Verse*

19—: An Elegy

◊　◊　◊

Apollo. Bebe Rebozo. Beatniks.
The Car. Counting backwards.
Cold Warriors. The century
I was born in. Disney. The Great
Depression and Anti-Depressants.
Everest. The Evil Empire. Electric
light and atomic energy. Frost
at Kennedy's Inaugural. Fucking.
Free love. Gridlock. Harley-Davidson
and Hell's Angels. *Ho Ho Ho Chi Minh.*
The Ivory-billed woodpecker. The Iron
Curtain. Joke: How many right-wing
neo-conservative, conspiracy theory,
survivalist, NRA, MIA, VFW,
free-market, anti-establishment
radio talk show host-loving loners
does it take to screw in a light bulb?
The Killing fields. Love-Beads.
Love-Ins. Love Canal. The Mall
of America. Medical waste. Richard
Nixon. No one's home. The century
when oral sex came into its own.
The overdose. *People.* Peaceniks.
Plutonium. Post-. Pop-. Plastic-wrapped
bundles of cocaine washing up
on Florida beaches. Queer theory.
Race. A small car like a stereo
on wheels, the Soul-Singer's voice
tearing through paper speaker cones

the way the spirit is formed and deformed
by the flesh. The century of the Teenager.
Televangelists. Uncut. Unadulterated.
Vietnam. Watergate. World Wars. The X-ray.
Yeah Yeah Yeah. Zen Koran. Grown Zero.

from *Michigan Quarterly Review*

I Need to Be More French. Or Japanese.

◇ ◇ ◇

Then I wouldn't prefer the California wine,
its big sugar, big fruit rolling down my tongue,
a cornucopia spilled across a tacky tablecloth.
I'd prefer the French, its smoke and rot.
Said Cézanne: *Le monde—c'est terrible!*
Which means, *The world—it bites the big weenie.*
People sound smarter in French.
The Japanese prefer the crescent moon to the full,
prefer the rose before it blooms.
Oh, I have been to the temples of Kyoto,
I have stood on the Pont Neuf, and my eyes,
they drank it in, but my taste buds
shuffled along in the beer line at Wrigley Field.
It was the day they gave out foam fingers.
I hereby pledge to wear more gray, less yellow
of the beaks of baby mockingbirds,
that huge yellow yawping open on wobbly necks,
trusting something yummy will be dropped inside,
soon. I hereby pledge to be reserved.
When the French designer learned
I didn't like her mockups for my book cover,
she sniffed, *They're not for everyone. They're
subtle. What area code is 662 anyway?* I said,
*Mississippi, sweetheart. Bet you couldn't find it
with a map.* Okay: I didn't really. But so what
if I'm subtle as May in Mississippi, my nose

in the wine-bowl of this magnolia bloom, so what
if I'm mellow as the punch-drunk bee.
If I were Japanese I'd write about magnolias
in March, how tonal, each bud long as a pencil,
sheathed in celadon suede, jutting from a cluster
of glossy leaves. I'd end the poem before anything
bloomed, end with rain swelling the buds
and the sheaths bursting, then falling to the grass
like a fairy's castoff slippers, like candy wrappers,
like spent firecrackers. Yes, my poem
would end there, spent firecrackers.
If I were French, I'd capture post-peak, in July,
the petals floppy, creased brown with age,
the stamens naked, stripped of yellow filaments.
The bees lazy now, bungling the ballet, thinking
for the first time about October. If I were French,
I'd prefer this, end with the red-tipped filaments
scattered on the scorched brown grass,
and my poem would incite the sophisticated,
the French and the Japanese readers—
because the filaments look like matchsticks,
and it's matchsticks, we all know, that start the fire.

from *Ploughshares*

EDWARD FIELD

In Praise of My Prostate

◊   ◊   ◊

While most men I know are having theirs irradiated,
scooped out, or surgically removed,
we're enjoying a blissful Indian Summer.

The more horror stories I hear
the more I'm determined to hold on to you—
you're my own and I want you just the way you are.

Yes, I pee all night like any guy my age,
and if I'm rarely rock hard anymore,
I'm not complaining—

rock hard's often numb as a stone
whereas you're a living bulb,
if bulbously encrusted by our long voyage.

and you still expand, your amazing flowers
bursting forth throughout my body,
pistils and stamens dancing.

from *Hanging Loose*

RICHARD GARCIA

Adam and Eve's Dog

◊   ◊   ◊

Not many people know it but Adam and Eve had a dog.
Its name was Kelev Reeshon, which means, first dog.
Some scholars say it had green fur and ate only plants
and grasses, and that is why some dogs still like to eat grass.
Other say it was hairless like the Chihuahua. Some
say it was male, some female, or that it was androgynous
like the angels or the present-day hyena. Rabbi Peretz,
a medieval cabalist in Barcelona, thought it was a black
dog and that it could see the angels which were everywhere
in the garden, although Adam and Eve could not see them.
He writes in his book of mystical dream meditations,
The Sefer Halom, that Kelev tried to help Adam and Eve
see the angels by pointing at them with its nose, aligning
its tail in a straight line with its back and raising one paw.
But Adam and Eve thought Kelev was pointing at the birds.
All scholars agree that it had a white tip on its tail,
and that it was a small dog. Sometimes you see
paintings of Eve standing next to a tree holding an apple.
The misinterpretation of this iconography gave birth
to the legend of the forbidden fruit and the fall from grace.
Actually, it was not an apple, but Kelev's ball and Eve
was about to throw it. One day, although there were no
days or nights as we know them, she threw the ball
right out of the garden. Kelev ran after it and did not return.
Adam and Eve missed their dog, but were afraid to leave
the garden. It was misty and dark outside the garden.
They could hear Kelev barking, always farther
and farther away, its bark echoing as if there were two dogs barking.
Finally, they could stand it no longer, and they gathered

Kelev's bed of large leaves and exited the garden.
They were holding the leaves in front of their bodies.
Although they could not see it, an angel followed,
trying to light up the way with a flaming sword.
And the earth was without form outside the garden.
Everything was gray and without shape or outline
because nothing outside the garden had a name. Slowly,
they advanced toward the sound of barking,
holding each other, holding their dog's bed against their bodies.
Eventually they made out something small and white,
swinging from side to side; it seemed to be leading them
through the mist into a world that was becoming more visible.
Now there were trees, and beneath their feet, there was a path.

from *Notre Dame Review*

Watch

◇ ◇ ◇

Yesterday, your tired wife and I
drove to the medical examiner's
to retrieve your personal effects.
She dropped me off at the front
entrance. The women at work
in that bland flat-roofed building
looked like secretaries at various
high schools you were principal
of over the last thirty years. The
back room was being remodeled,
so ideal placement of FAX
machines and the shredder
were under discussion. An older
woman with dyed blonde hair
searched the property closet twice
for your watch. "It's here on the
computer," she said, shaking
her head, "but I can't locate it
on the premises." She phoned
the exam room to see if they still
had it "down there." Finally, on her
third trip to the closet, she found it.
I signed for the sealed, formaldehyde
smelling plastic bag, a form printed
on it in black ink. *Reason confiscated/
offense. Arresting officer/chain of custody.
Location where obtained.* The same form
for every crime, accident, fatality.
When I returned to the car, I found

your wife asleep at the wheel.
Not wanting to disturb her, I stood
and watched her awhile through
the rolled up window. What would
I give this waking minute, *my car
my house every book I ever owned*, trifles all,
to be able to kiss your brow and rouse
you now as if from a needed sleep?
I tore the bag open with my teeth.
It tasted awful. Inside, your everyday
watch with brown leather band, still ticking.

from *Sycamore Review*

Blue on Her Hands

◇ ◇ ◇

Most of the block is up. The laundromat's lit.
A man in a suit walking a dog.
Aikido students in light rain.
Automatic metal storefront folding.
The flower seller attending her bundles. Blue stain on her hands.
Glass faces buying time, coffee.
Imagine, striped tulips loosening in dark underground.
Nothing is final. When the train comes,
Get on board.

It seems simple on a night like this. The end of a mild Winter day, chill wind now,
Flapping whatever is loose in the dark, to understand how a boy from childhood
Wanted to mimic the rockets that shot off fireworks, and built a home-made one
That blew off three of his fingers. He is reminded of it every day.
You think of it only from time to time. You can understand
Everything fully, if that is your desire, especially on a night like this when
        everything is turning.
Everything comes from the taupe water, from the tongue. Knowledge. Love. I
        wanted to learn
Every part of you for a long time. Now, next to you,
There are white particles, tiny, adrift, in the dark.

The doctor questioned you about the dream. At least you thought she was a doctor.
She had a clipboard. She clicked a string of pearls that rested on her sweater and
        breasts.
How beautiful the afternoon dissolving into dusk outside the twentieth story.
        How could
You tell her all you could remember was a snapshot
(Pinned to the wall, that played no important part in the dream)

Of a nude, hand covering her sex, one of her fingers missing, or plunged into the
        mystery,
A pigeon feather loose on the quilt. You substituted a dream your son told you.
How you and your best friend were *locked up* by the police. How he and his
Mother trailed the police car. How you and your best friend could not
See the show. He and his mother trailed the police car in hopes of freeing you.
Your son furrowed his brow as he told you the dream, with more worry than
A four-year old deserves. *Mmm, interesting,* the doctor says. She wears dark stockings
You believe must smell like anise and earth. Half of what we eat grows
In sun, half rustles in loose dark soil. Mmm, interesting.

from *American Poetry Review*

JESSICA GOODHEART

Advice for a Stegosaurus

◊   ◊   ◊

Never mind the asteroid,
the hot throat of the volcano,
a sun that daily drops into the void.

Comb the drying riverbed for drink.
Strut your bird-hipped body.
Practice a lizard grin. Don't think.

Stretch out your tail. Walk, as you must,
in a slow deliberate gait.
Don't look back, Dinosaur. Dust is dust.

You'll leave your bones, your fossil feet
and armored eye-lids.
Put your chin to the wind. Eat what you eat.

from *The Antioch Review*

The Searchers

◇　◇　◇

Hangovers helped John Wayne evince deep torment
in *The Searchers*, when he comes unglued
while tracking the Comanches who've abducted
Natalie Wood. With Jeffrey Hunter as his
sidekick, he combs the empty wilderness
until the trail revolves into an odd

infinitude. The quest attains a sweeping,
cosmic grandeur as the wayworn pair
return repeatedly in VistaVision
to bust up certain funerals and weddings,
while, past the stone pavilions of the canyon,
Natalie Wood still pines, a captive squaw.

Of course she's later rescued and returned
and it's John Wayne who finally is forced
to drift along the dreary plain alone.
And Jeffrey Hunter (much beloved of Frank
O'Hara) went on to play the role of Christ,
as well as anyone has, in *King of Kings*,

where Nick Ray made him stay inside his trailer
so he could smoke unseen by other cast
members, and extras would be awed by him
when he came on the set. Jeff shaved his armpits
for the Crucifixion, knowing well
the Lord must suffer in ideality,

mounted high and gleaming on the Cross,
a waxed and buff Apollo crowned with thorns.
It was the end, really, of Jeff's career,
banished to foreign features and depressed,
then suddenly dead at forty-three in obscure
circumstances, having fallen down a staircase.

from *Court Green*

The Turn of the Screw

◇   ◇   ◇

The biggest influence on me, thanks for asking,
was James: *The Turn of the Screw*. Back in the service kitchen,
I've got a fiancé ruined by it, the tower,
the burning womanly pond, thank god, all her palm-fronds
turn me on, my nudie life drawing model. I got that yearning
from James, a servant you can count on to do her duty,
spurn a child raving in the night and acting slyboots
so she can come to my bed and make headway, on so bookish.
I got the night from James, but not the dew, and not the sentence—
his churn and churn, a ribbon through some actress'
brilliantly emotive red vagina, the kind that chews the scenery.
My fiancé won't watch the movie as she makes the household stew,
how innocent the young charges act, as if they never swam home,
how the public part of the novella made it plain:
how it influenced me, gave me what to do,
made me its steward, learned me what for, asked me to marry.

from *American Letters & Commentary*

For Kateb Yacine

(Algerian playwright, novelist, poet,
and activist, 1929–89)

◊   ◊   ◊

A moment jumps the interval; the next
second, a sudden dissonance swells up,
a crack down the smooth surface of the cup,
a dialogue with mistranslated text,
a tense the narrative poises, perplexed,
upon. The dancers and the singer stop,
swirled, each, in shadow like a velvet cape,
potential, and ambiguously sexed.
A gender and a nationality
implicit in the ululation rise
from a long throat to claim or compromise
privilege; responsibility
in texture, in that wound of sound, that vexed
surface, which could detonate, could drop.

Could drop into the anonymity
of headlines: war and fear and fear of war
and war abetted by ambient fear
honed to a hunger by publicity.
But there is a room above the street, a three-
o'clock winter sun, the nuanced, near-
ly translucent voice of a counter-tenor
threading a cantata by Scarlatti.
There were the exile's words in Arabic
anathematizing any deity

if slaughter is sanctified in its name;
the voice, the struggle from which words became
corporeally transformed to music.
There is the emblematic cup of tea.

There is the emblematic pot of tea
steaming on a wooden bench between
antagonists engaged in conversation
halfway to official enmity,
halfway to some compromise they can agree
upon, and not lose face. A city drones
and screeches in the crepuscule beyond
the room, in contrapuntal energy.
They keep sentences moving, savor the way
to pluck the pertinent or flabby phrase
and skin and gut it, twisting in the air:
a game they magisterially play
like diplomats, not gray-sweatered, gray-haired
exiles filling the breach of winter days.

Exiles filling the breath of winter days
with rhetoric have nothing, but have time
for rhetoric as logical as rhyme.
Meanwhile a speechwriter drafts the ukase
which, broadcast to a military base,
sends children and their city up in flames.
Meanwhile, an editor collects our names
and texts in protest: we can only guess
who else is keeping tabs, who else will be
pilloried in an op-ed in the *Times*,
distracted by brief notoriety
or told a passport will not be renewed.
Imagined exiles, with what gratitude
I'd follow your riposted paradigms.

To make of his riposte a paradigm,
he conjured Nedjma from the wilderness
behind his distance-mined electric face.
Kahina, Nedjma, Amnıa, a woman's name

ejaculated to a stadium:
a heroine, a first lover unseen
for decades, a mother who mimed, silence upon
women's silence screamed past millennium.
Another silence, the interlocutor
who argued over wine with Paul Celan
until the words were not German or French
in the cold hypothesis of the Seine,
no longer comforter, companion, tutor
to the last Jew on the November bench.

If the last Jew on the November bench
shivered, rose, walked to the rue de Tournon
and ordered a Rémy and a *ballon*
de rouge with Roth, could it blot out the stench
of ash and lies for both? (Over the ranch
in Texas what smoke rises in premon-
itory pillar?) The gaunt Algerian
asynchronous, among them, needs to quench
an equal thirst. We all had pseudonyms,
code-names, pet-names, pen-names: *noms de guerre*,
simple transliterations, unfamiliar
diphthongs in rote order, palindromes
and puns patched on the untranslatable
(unuttered, anguished) root of a syllable.

Unuttered, anguished, roots of a syllable
in her first language threaded the page she'd sign
(written at night, in a strange town, hidden
among strangers, once betrayed) "Nicole
Sauvage."*
            Sun gilds the roof of the town hall,
its bridal parties gone, too cold, too late.
The February sky is celibate,
precipitated towards a funeral.

*"Nicole Sauvage" was the pseudonym used by the writer Nathalie Sarraute during
the Nazi occupation of France during World War II, in the village where she went into
hiding with her daughters after being denounced as a Jew by neighbors in another village.

Yes, war will come and we will demonstrate;
war will come and reams of contraband
reportage posted on the Internet
will flesh out censored stories, secondhand.
Tire-treads lumbering towards its already-fixed
moment jump the interval: this war, the next.

from *New England Review* and *PN Review*

I May After Leaving You Walk Quickly or Even Run

◊　◊　◊

Rain fell in a post-Romantic way.
Heads in the planets, toes tucked

under carpets, that's how we got our bodies
through. The translator made the sign

for twenty horses backing away from
a lump of sugar. Yes, you.

When I said did you want me
I meant me in the general sense.

The drink we drank was cordial.
In a spoon, the ceiling fan whirled.

The Old World smoked in the fireplace.
Glum was the woman in the ostrich feather hat.

from *88*

Contributors' Notes

◊   ◊   ◊

STACEY HARWOOD lives in Paris, where she teaches at La Varenne. She is credited with reviving the artisanal bread movement when she opened a tiny boulangerie, Pain Fermier on Rue Christine in the 6th Arrondissement. Her essays and recipes have appeared in *Journal of Gastronomy, Gourmet, L'Art Culinaire,* and numerous magazines both here and abroad. Her book, *Stalking the Wild Yeast,* based on her Food Network program of the same name, is forthcoming from Workingman Press.

STACEY HARWOOD is the founder and executive director of Warm Hands for the Homeless, a not-for-profit organization in Boston that recruits nursing-home residents from fourteen cities throughout the United States and Canada to knit mittens for the homeless from donated yarn-mill overruns. She was awarded a MacArthur Fellowship or "genius" grant in 1992.

STACEY HARWOOD is a third-year student at University of Michigan Law School. She appears as Bryanna on the HBO series *G-String Divas.* Her poetry and fiction have appeared in *Herotica, Yellow Silk, Switch/bitch* and *GASH.com.*

STACEY HARWOOD breeds and trains German shepherds on his farm in Eden, New York, a suburb of Buffalo where his family has farmed for three generations. He teaches composition at Erie Community College. His essays have appeared in *Men's World, Outside, Southern Quarterly Review, Creative Nonfiction,* the *New York Times Magazine,* and elsewhere. His work has twice been selected for inclusion in the annual *Best of the Small Presses* anthology (HarperCollins, 1989, 1995). His memoir, *Come, Sit, Stay,* is due next spring.

STACEY HARWOOD received a Golden Globe award for her screen-play adaptation of Alberto Moravia's *Conjugal Love*. She is making her directorial debut this fall with a film based on the life of Italo Svevo (Ettore Schmitz) and his time in Trieste.

RABBI SHAYNA RACHEL HOROWITZ lives in Philadelphia where she and her husband are assistant rabbis at Congregation Beth-Shalom. This is her first publication.

Ever since foiling a hijacking attempt during a transatlantic flight, STACEY HARWOOD has been a motivational speaker.

STACEY HARWOOD was born in 1936. She teaches dance interpre-tation at Sarah Lawrence College. Harwood performed with Katherine Dunham's Chicago workshop before an injury ended her promising dance career. Harwood is the author of numerous works of poetry, fic-tion, and nonfiction, most recently *Closing in on the Light* (Knopf, 1998), which was the recipient of the first-ever Lifetime Extraordinary Achievement Award given by the International Society of Artists, Writ-ers, and Performers.

Of "Contributors' Notes," Harwood writes: "I have long been inter-ested in exploring the boundaries of identity and gender among certain marginalized groups. When I was no longer able to do this through dance, I turned for survival to words. Just as there is joy and sadness in knowing who you are, so too is there joy and sadness—no grief—in knowing who you are not. This poem arises out of my musings on the limits of temporal experience as provoked by cultural constraints."

from *LIT*

Variations on Two Black Cinema Treasures

◊   ◊   ◊

1. "BROKEN EARTH"
Year of Release: 1939
Running Time: 11 minutes
Cast: Clarence Muse and unidentified boy

I am the sick boy in the shack, when the camera opens
On the sunrise and wispy silhouettes of the plow
And the fool mule and my father working a row down

The middle of a rock field with a small shack in one corner
And a shade tree in the other where a crew of barefoot

Old black men stoop and sing "All God's Chillun Wear Shoes"
And call out *Hey* and *Hi* and the name of my father
Who goes on plowing into sundown, into the dark hour

When the mule will grunt no farther and the red eyes
Of the black men's cigarettes blaze and flicker in one corner

Of the field as I quiver in a wet skin in the hot small light
Of the lantern blazing and flickering in the shack.
I am a sick boy. I am as still as a kettle of water. I am waiting

To be rearranged by the hand of God, which is not the hand
Of God, but the strip of cloth pressed against my brow

By my father who has no medicine but prayer.
I don't now what I did to get here mumbling
"Pappy" and calling out to the ghost of my mother

As a choir sings "Swing Low, Sweet Chariot" somewhere.
I don't know who it is telling me to open my eyes.

II. "BOOGIE WOOGIE BLUES"
      Year of Release: 1948
      Running Time: 10 minutes
      Cast: vocalist and pianist Hadda Brooks performing three songs

If you have slept in a house made of nothing but a smile
That drooped around your neck like a five pound chain;
If you have whittled all the virtuous words in the Bible down

To *Amen* the way pillow talk can be whittled down to a tongue,
You know the name of my song: "Don't Take Your Love from Me."

Don't take your love away from me. Your house key.
Your toothbrush. Your swing and sweet scripture
Of touching and preacher's breath. Don't take your fingertips

And hunger from my ears. I know the lyrics
Of the oldest love song: "Don't You Think I Ought to Know."

Don't you think I out to know, Baby, the doctrine of the Blues,
The spells and fevers of the Blues, the Blues' epistemologies?
I know the lyrics of the oldest love songs. And the new ones too.

Why bother rise and dress now that you are gone?
Why bother boogie woogie? "I'm Tired of Everything but You."

from *CROWD*

Seesaws

◇　◇　◇

The bigger the tomb, the smaller the man.
The weaker the case, the thicker the brief.
The deeper the pain, the older the wound.
The graver the loss, the dryer the tears.

The truer the shot, the slower the aim.
The quicker the kiss, the sweeter the taste.
The viler the crime, the vaguer the guilt.
The louder the price, the cheaper the ring.

The higher the climb, the sheerer the slide.
The steeper the odds, the shrewder the bet.
The rarer the chance, the brasher the risk.
The colder the snow, the greener the spring.

The braver the bull, the wiser the cape.
The shorter the joke, the surer the laugh.
The sadder the tale, the dearer the joy.
The longer the life, the briefer the years.

from *The Atlantic Monthly*

Motes

◊   ◊   ◊

A mote it is to trouble
the mind's eye.

They wandered out of gloom
Into some golden shaft
Of late afternoon light,
Those tiny filaments
That filled me with delight,
Lifted by an updraft
Or viewless influence
There in the living room.

They might be minuscule
Angels, it seemed to me,
Needing no wings to rise
Or slide back out of sight
But floating effortlessly
Through our interior skies,
Each incandescent mite
A pilot at flight school.

Their rises, their declines,
Resembled Jacob's dream
And seemed an allegory
Enacted just for me
There in my own sunbeam
But swathed in mystery—
Some esoteric story
Wrought in encoded signs:

One more of the shrewd, well-tried
Ways that a child is kept
From some shrouded, grown-up truth,
Probably linked with tears;
For the one thing clear to youth
Is that no joy goes unwept,
And that their utmost fears
Will be amply justified;

Which makes them minor sages,
Without the words for what
They cannot yet know or say:
That whatever lies in store,
They were type-cast in some play
With a far from comic plot—
Grief, selfishness, and war
Crowding its dog-eared pages.

from *The New Yorker*

The Propagation of the Species

◇　◇　◇

It is likely that someone
will be standing there at the end
of time, looking up at the fireball
or down at the organs of desire.

It won't be us, but only because odds
are odds: uncanny, cranky, spare. Thus
we may judge the world a safe
enough place. These are the cares
of the day, the age of probability
having replaced historic ne'er-do-wells
with numbers. As for us, we live in
surprise; why not share this mood
and facial disposition with some scion
of the future generation?

We spent our meditation-time instead
confessing. The exercise delivered
unexpected fruit. Perhaps we've better quarry
than the truth.

The fruit of all of this is
possession and release,
mango and bananas.

Especially bananas. Try expressing
to a friend, when next you are feeling
unglued or blue, say: *I'm bananas.* Explain
to others that your lover, while very

sweet and handsomely randy, is a mite *bananas*;
is bananas. With a meaningful look in your eye,
gesture an unpeeling.

It is your autobiography
you are living. The actor eating scampi
to my left says he is not yet off-book, but
will be. Folks, I am ever-so-slightly off-book;
Friends, I am bananas.

We parse the problem, nouning out the principle
players: friends, families, prospects. I interview
the possibility of a child;
ask it questions. Intone the word: *Interested?*
Then: *Want to learn the word for widget?*
Want to read Beowulf? Want to get named?

Shall we grin and bear it?
I admit, existence is where *woeful*
was conjured. Nonetheless, to recommend it,
there is Jell-O; average rainfall; the anchovy
app at Luna's; and the fact that in the middle, many
change their minds on the whole shebang—get
a good one off in both directions. But you and I
are going to have to choose.

It is our autobiography
we are eating; you snooze you
lose. Still, in the midst of going too slowly,
all hell was been known to break loose.

A gang of snails attacks a tree sloth, steals her wallet.
Down at the station, police chief
questions: *How'd they get ya?*
Sloth says, *I dunno, it happened so fast.*

Ain't it the truth. All this wallowing
in the details of engagement
and when the battle comes,
it isn't quite expected. It's slower. Also,

over much too fast to make a fair
assessment. Lounging in her tea tree,
chewing leaves and dreaming, she sees
them: tiny, slimy things with spiral shells
and damp antennae that float like sea anemone
above their wet-tongue heads. She wonders
softly: Is it a moment for decision?

Shall I bolt or battle? Or better yet,
might this pass me by without regret?
It took days for the battalion
to cross the stretch of trunk and reach
her, yet she was still mulling it over
when she found herself succumbed.
Years later, still on her way home
from the station, she wondered what
she had wanted with a wallet, anyway.

There is no way to parry ordinary disaster.
There are no odds worth playing.

Animal-stars from early motion-pictures
eat bonbons and wear feathered mules
in their trailers; the old-age home; the zoo.
What, on the other hand, will become
of you and I?

Side by side, the Studebakers inside us
ride along the Côte du Rhone,
our hair getting tangled in the violent wind of speed.

And how do you propose we un-knot
all these tangles? Not, I trust,
on the rocks below: brave souls pick
a hotel from the travel guide and go.

What do fools do? Don't know.
Probably the same but badly.
Bombardiers stay home. Bombardiers
know too much of bombs to roam.

Still, it is a question of the result
of one's actions. Mendel was a monk,
watching pea-pods, but had a wild effect
on pillow talk in centuries to follow;
mumblings of the pregnant engineer.

What do you get from a threesome of a tiger,
a scorpion, and a fly?

Bumble-bee.
How do you get a zebra? Mix a horse
and a tiger.
How you get a tiger? Mix a lion
with that same zebra from before.

Let us accept a rainy August day
as if it were a single, unlikely fabrication.
As if these movies had
never been on television before, as if we'd
never heard of Mamie Eisenhower,
as if her tiny bangs could still cause us to smile.

The recovering tree sloth hangs upside-down,
her three-toed feet hooked to the fat branch
above her as she lollingly observes
the tropic scene. *Much,* she muses,
to which we cling, turns out to be . . .
ah well. She's lost her train of thought,
chewing a mild leaf and swinging gently
with the breeze.

Odds of the home-front; odds of the sun;
odds of a herringbone. Run, run, run.

from *In Posse Review*

from The Fatalist

◇   ◇   ◇

There was a message. I gave it
to you, you passed it to me, I returned it, and now you have given it
to me among others cascading like a million peas
from a thousand pods to the floor with hideous exactitude.
"Duck the pot shot, fuck the hot shot," said the doctor to her soldiers
but they had heard the joke before in other friendships
forced by jokes. The lab technician came out
and, glancing at the sign-in sheet, said "Ms. Cunningham?" Both
the white woman and the black woman stood. Furthermore
they were both school teachers able to swim through steel
with their skepticism digging a hole for the truck
to dump sand into. The driver triumphantly stretched
his hands into the air and shouted a grand affirmation: "NO!"

★

The best words get said frequently—they are like fertile pips.
Apples fall heavily to the ground and lie in the sun, their scent
abandoning them as a philosophy which cannot be further perfected. Love
releases playful sensations even from serious things providing a life
to think about. Take R—the only thing
R could credit herself with was having lived
her life and so she not only kept an account of it
but did so not in the privacy of a diary but in the form of letters
—abundant, profligate, indiscreet—that I want to write
to you so as to note something that I read
this morning: "It's not that this or that means something
to *me* but that *this!*—or *that!*—means something to me." Musically
R bequeaths herself to posterity as a scholar might

bequeath his or her library blowing twisted veils of rain
past the narrow and curving windows in the last hour that will carry us along
to the time when those who come after us will learn
what we know—a man with a mustache waxed and dyed
green, a line of tall people and a woman at the door, a committee
of children without scooters but not mournful, a poet with a motive, a pilot
with a flashlight, a sulking but fascinated scholar, and Goethe
no doubt for whom R would have released a flock of red canaries.

*

If it's light, it is day, if it's day, it is light and the high heavens
bobbing on the surface of the sea *are* the surface of the sea
and that should be their name as the wind lifts it
giving it *its* name, the one that lets us see how like a bunch of grapes
we are when practicing meterology. A lucid thinker
needs some names. Rosie? Soren? Certainly
reality provides the materials
from which the imagination can concoct what it cares about.
Of course it would be useful to have different means
for describing different projects if we could keep them straight
beginning with the bottom one which shows the androgynous child
staring out from a pink landscape that is all horizon
with a calla lily. Hallucinations are always possible
and currently likely. I got up this morning
hoping maybe that would help me get ahead of the game
but already before it was my turn I was asking "What game?"
and the only answer was "This one." Now I have to ask "Is it fun
if played?" Everything that is played is
somewhat accidental and this game is committed
to heterogeneity, maintaining the otherness of what it does
out of respect for the otherness that distinguishes the world we share
with others. I've begun. Your turn comes next
but you could wait until another emergency arises and instigates another
assignment meant to get citizens to reflect analytically on the parts of life
toward the end of the sequence that are anti-lyrics, dystopic
and dysphoric. Feel free. I can't imagine
enduring weather that heats a day to 121 degrees, the living inert
while things get noisy, snapping in the underbrush, bark
buzzing, thefts occurring

without thieves over the next few weeks if not exactly as I'd hoped
at least well enough, thanks.

★

The children now admit that they are violent. Let's lodge them
in philosophy until their house is built. I like the tether
and send a message to a fugitive more and more
taken by the nightingale's information which is all about
the desperately ungraspable vastness of meaning
everywhere and the fact that as flesh and blood
mortals we are doomed always to lose meaning
for lack of adverbs. Meanwhile we are slowly to lay out our differences.
Language writing rejects the notion of genius
and the New York School embraces it, I am sure,
it is somewhere here in the room, D said so, but so are paper breads
and notebook cheeses. And truth be told, Hans Christian Andersen
has done things with the Danish language that no one
before or since has been able to do. Chefs and foodies
may fly in from all over the world, Martha Stewart may be there
but only two photographers will be allowed to play tapes
of poets reading poems and in particular tapes of Gertrude Stein doing so.
Of course. The most popularly demanded goods are always those
of perfect quality. The cheerful woman in the yellow scarf strides
toward us bearing towels. Her new bicycle was a floor model,
but it is strong and she is fast
and dexterous enough to go on
as long as the streets provide her with a theater for exaggeration.

from *BOMB*

Remorse
After a Panic Attack
in a Wisconsin Field, 1975

◊   ◊   ◊

In the grasses, waving above the stricken aunt,
Ann with her small hands
Patted and smoothed, like the mother
The aunt never had.

To fall, the aunt had picked a site
Bordered with poison ivy
Thick by the roadside—Ann strode through
And led her aunt out.

The aunt's knees had buckled—
A combination of fear and decrepitude
Aided by the omni-bottle.

Why should everyone live like you,
Ruth? Why should they bother?

I stoutly maintain the absence of God,
And expect those nestling at His breast
To congratulate my ardor.

Why should everyone live like you,
Ruth? Why should they bother?

I talk rivalry of siblings
In the midst of the cult of family.
I decry deepfreezes
To those who catalog viands.

If someone says something pleasant
I correct their misapprehension.
I see threats and violence stalking
Among grasses and apples,
Football games and cards.
I am the specter at the feast,
The spoiler of marshmallow roasts.

And everyone must be like me.
Ruth. Everyone must bother.

from *New Letters*

Burlap Sack

◇ ◇ ◇

A person is full of sorrow
the way a burlap sack is full of stones or sand.
We say, "Hand me the sack,"
but we get the weight.
Heavier if left out in the rain.
To think that the stones or sand are the self is an error.
To think that grief is the self is an error.
Self carries grief as a pack mule carries the side bags,
being careful between the trees to leave extra room.
The mule is not the load of ropes and nails and axes.
The self is not the miner nor builder nor driver.
What would it be to take the bride
and leave behind the heavy dowry?
To let the thin-ribbed mule browse in tall grasses,
its long ears waggling like the tails of two happy dogs?

from *Runes*

In a Quiet Town by the Sea

◊   ◊   ◊

Once I listened to two guys talk about fucking around.
One of them said he liked to meet someone
in a city far away from where he lives
and to get her into the strange clean sheets of a hotel bed.

He said skin was the holiest testament of all
and that to remove the clothes of a sexualized stranger

was like filling your lungs with oxygen
before diving into the swimming pool of god.

He said, Pleasure doesn't care
whose cup you drink it from—
and you could tell it was something he had read once in a book,
written down and practiced in his head.

The other guy said that the stink from secrets in a marriage
was like the smell of decomposing flesh
rising from under the foundation of your house.

He said love is writing your name in cement,

and anyway his wife would know in a NASCAR minute
if he came home with the smell of pussy on his clothes.

There were drinks on the table of course
and a blonde waitress buzzing around
like the goddess of temptation in a budget film
—whose breasts, silhouetted in her blouse,

were like exhibits A and B in the impending criminal case
—as she herself was clearly
destined to be evidence
for both the defense and prosecution.

And there was something so typical about these guys
with their alcohol and self-glorifying memories,

their longing to conquer the world
and yet to still be coddled by their mommy-wives,

you wanted to have them dipped in plastic for a keychain,
or to turn to the salesman and say,
Can we see something a little, no, please, something *completely* different?

Outside the moon gazed upon the earth with wary ardor;
the church cast its shadow upon the plaza
like a triangle and square
in a troubling geometry problem. . . .

And in the houses and the neighborhoods, it's distressing to report,
there was no one sleeping. There was no one sleeping
who did not dream of being touched.

from *The Cincinnati Review*

Ants

◇   ◇   ◇

Ants are not fond of margarine. Like us they prefer
Butter. They do not have cholesterol problems
Because as yet they do not own TVs. For centuries
They have toiled in order that they might be able to
Take a night off and watch the Northern Lights which
Are their version of canned laughter. They hate picnics
But feel compelled by folklore to attend them
Or at minimum do a drive by chicken leg grab. Their
Queen is a pain in the ass. They don't love her but
Without her they would be common, so they serve her.
She is an insatiable nymphomaniac but they don't
Hold that against her trying instead to stay busy with work.
Forgotten ancient languages have been genetically
Imprinted in them at birth and they say things they
Don't understand. Like us they often make bad marriages.
But because of their outstanding physical prowess
And humility there is seldom cause for divorce. They
Haven't read the great philosophers but they know them
Innately. They love the flowers of Spring and lacking
Perspective eagerly run all over them. They
Are much like us. They are nudists but because Puritanism
Has not invaded their genetic code, it does not
Affect their work ethic and each ant loves its own body.
Therefore they don't care about go-go boots and
Sandals. Like us, Ants are driven by their hearts and pretend
That it is all in the name of duty. Ants are never impulsive.
When they laugh, the gardens of old maids tremble. Ants
Love to dance but lack a sense of rhythm so

They gave it up when Homer scorned them. Rain is their
Sensuality. It makes them feel delirious and late. Quivering
And running between rain drops to their fate.

from *Mudfish*

DONALD JUSTICE

A Chapter in the Life
of Mr. Kehoe, Fisherman

◊   ◊   ◊

Some nights on the dock,
When only scales
And a few popeyed fish-heads
Are left out for the moon
(Which the spread nets entangle),
There comes the sound
Of bare feet dancing,
Which is Mr. Kehoe,
Lindying solo,
Whirling, dipping
In his long skirt
That swells and billows,
Turquoise and pink,
Mr. Kehoe in sequins,
Face turned upward,
Eyes half-shut, dreaming.

Sleep well, Mr. Kehoe.

from *The New Criterion*

MARY KARR

A Blessing from
My Sixteen Years' Son

◊ ◊ ◊

I have this son who assembled inside me
during Hurricane Gloria. In a flash, he appeared,
in a heartbeat. Outside, pines toppled.

Phone lines snapped and hissed like cobras.
Inside, he was a raw pearl: microscopic, luminous.
Look at the muscled obelisk of him now

pawing through the icebox for more grapes.
Sixteen years and not a bone broken,
not a single stitch. By his age,

I was marked more ways, and small.
He's a slouching six foot three,
with implausible blue eyes, which settle

on the pages of Emerson's "Self-Reliance"
with profound belligerence.
A girl with a navel ring

could make his cell phone go *brr*,
or an Afro'd boy leaning on a mop at Taco Bell—
creatures strange as dragons or eels.

Balanced on a kitchen stool, each gives counsel
arcane as any oracle's. Bruce claims school
is harshing my mellow. Case longs to date

a tattooed girl, because he wants a woman
willing to do stuff she'll regret.
They've come to lead my son

into his broadening spiral.
Someday soon, the tether
will snap. I birthed my own mom

into oblivion. The night my son smashed
the car fender, then rode home
in the rain-streaked cop car, he asked, *Did you*

and Dad screw up so much?
He'd let me tuck him in,
my grandmother's wedding quilt

from 1912 drawn to his goateed chin. *Don't*
blame us, I said. *You're your own*
idiot now. At which he grinned.

The cop said the girl in the crimped Chevy
took it hard. He'd found my son
awkwardly holding her in the canted headlights,

where he'd draped his own coat
over her shaking shoulders. *My fault,*
he'd confessed right off.

Nice kid, said the cop.

from *The New Yorker*

Hell and Love

◇　◇　◇

Hell is always grander to paint
Than the bliss of a resurrected saint;
More fun to show the lecher's doom,
Tits and ass in the flicking gloom.

Yet love inspires more than hate,
A head caressed than on a plate,
And even should his colors wash,
I'd put Chagall in front of Bosch.

The Passion is a painter's dream,
With hell and love a single theme—
The human body stripped to show
A death both merciful and slow.

from *Image*

The Wolf

◇　◇　◇

The diseased dog lowered her head as I came close, as if to make
Of her head a shadow, something that the next few hours
Would erase, swiftly, something of no account. And what came
To mind was the she wolf who, beneath the wild fig, nursed
The twins that would build what amounted to a lasting city
On this earth. And it was as if, on that hot afternoon, I was standing
Not in the empty aisle between the gardens that have been
Reduced to nothing except the most rudimentary plants
And the eroding outlines of brick walls and barren terraces
But in the white hot light of a studio, in which a sculptor,
Working from the only model he has, a poor dog, is carving
Out of the blackest of black stones a female wolf with two rows
Of triangular tits that look like the twin rows of cedars the dog
Swam through and from which two boys, fat-thighed
And fated, are suspended. And the truth is both wolf and dog
Are ancient, for the sick dog comes not from the garden
But from another time, in another city, a sabbath day, foreign,
The street absolutely empty, the day shapely around me,
The houses, the walks, all ordered and white, and then
Out of the ordered whiteness proceeds a thing of great disorder,
A shape from the world of shadows, something to drive
Away. But I did not drive her away, though I could do
Nothing for her. And now I would make of her something
Better than she could make of herself. Though the wolf
Is only remembered in her prime, and not as she must
Have been years later, after all that would pass had passed.

from *32 Poems*

Shelley

◊ ◊ ◊

When I was twenty the one true
free spirit I had heard of was Shelley,
Shelley, who wrote tracts advocating
atheism, free love, the emancipation
of women, the abolition of wealth and class,
and poems on the bliss of romantic love,
Shelley, who, I learned later, perhaps
almost too late, remarried Harriet,
then pregnant with their second child,
and a few months later ran off with Mary,
already pregnant herself, bringing
with them Mary's stepsister Claire,
who very likely also became his lover,

and in this malaise à trois, which Shelley
had imagined would be "a paradise of exiles,"
they lived, along with the spectre of Harriet,
who drowned herself in the Serpentine,
and of Mary's half sister Fanny,
who killed herself, maybe for unrequited
love of Shelley, and with the spirits
of adored but often neglected
children conceived incidentally
in the pursuit of Eros—Harriet's
Ianthe and Charles, denied to Shelley
and consigned to foster parents; Mary's
Clara, dead at one; her Willmouse,
Shelley's favorite, dead at three; Elena,
the baby in Naples, almost surely

Shelley's own, whom he "adopted"
and then left behind, dead at one and a half;
Allegra, Claire's daughter by Byron,
whom Byron sent off to the convent
at Bagnacavallo at four, dead at five—

and in those days, before I knew
any of this, I thought I followed Shelley,
who thought he was following radiant desire.

from *The New Yorker*

In the Graveyard
of Fallen Monuments

◇   ◇   ◇

Moscow, near Gorky Park

Sometimes I like to think about Leonid Brezhnev
whose white marble torso stands here dreaming

in the Graveyard of Fallen Monuments. Leonid,
I say, it's Dick. Where are your goddamn legs?

Seems like yesterday you broke out the Stoli
at your dacha, and we laughed about détente.

Those were good times. The world on a razor
of our mutually assured destruction, and yet—

comrade! you remember—we felt strangely free.
Today not a single statue of Dick Nixon

stands astride an American city, but there are
National Guardsmen at the glittering bridges

and Citizen Corps tipsters behind each tree.
Leonid, they miss me. And the impoverished gray

pensioners in Gorky Park, endlessly pining
for "The Kuznetsk Metal Workers' Supper,"

they carry a wild red blowtorch for their Leonchik
too. So dosvidan'ya, you sweet old bastard—

I'm late to catch an Elks convention shambling
through my Library in Yorba Linda, California,

laden with cheap "Elvis Meets Nixon" keychains
and a queer uneasiness they cannot place.

from *Denver Quarterly* and *Poetry Daily*

Hell

◇　◇　◇

The second-hardest thing I have to do is not be longing's slave.

Hell is that. Hell is that, others, having a job, and not having a job. Hell is thinking continually of those who were truly great.

Hell is the moment you realize that you were ignorant of the fact, when it was true, that you were not yet ruined by desire.

The kind of music I want to continue hearing after I am dead is the kind that makes me think I will be capable of hearing it then.

There is music in Hell. Wind of desolation! It blows past the egg-eyed statues. The canopic jars are full of secrets.

The wind blows through me. I open my mouth to speak.

I recite the list of people I have copulated with. It does not take long. I say the names of my imaginary children. I call out four-syllable words beginning with B. This is how I stay alive.

Beelzebub. Brachiosaur. Bubble-headed. I don't know how I stay alive. What I do know is that there is a light, far above us, that goes out when we die,

and that in Hell there is a gray tulip that grows without any sun.
It reminds me of everything I failed at,

and I water it carefully. It is all I have to remind me of you.

from *Conduit*

Ill-Made Almighty

◇　◇　◇

No man has more assurance than a bad poet.
　　　　　　　　　　　　　—Martial

The logos thrives, it is crawling
with bugs. The lecturers, below,

are memorific, futurized, dead-certain
they'll go unsurprised. They don't

know nows as you do, true to no
clear destination. (You can't even act

your age, it's over-understudied.) Steady
as you go. The greatest waves are barely

bearable, alive's ill-read already,
and the Skipper is sick

of the terribly lit
graffiti in the head.

from *32 Poems* and *Verse Daily*

Space Marriage

◇ ◇ ◇

1

Our starship blew up
between Alpha Centaur
and the Second Quadrant
but we could not die
because we had stolen
the god's codes:

so we kept traveling
deeper into the future
just ahead of our bodies
and when we had sex

we felt ourselves scattering:
there in the galactic cold
where the immense numbers
begin to rotate slowly

we put on the robes
of the night sky.

2

An alien had imprisoned me
in that lunar module
that was just the thought
I and he fed me

what *I* would eat
and mated me
with the one *I* loved:

strange ordeal
there in the Second Quadrant
in Spica's radio-shadow
where the gravity of time
pulls dreams from a sleeper's mind:

bitter confinement
naked on a falling stone.

3

We built robots who built robots
that had a little of our hesitation,
our fatigue, our jealousy,
our longing for Alpha, peace, nonbeing . . .

They covered our long retreat,
those machines, that looked
like can-openers or outboard motors,
but with the guilty air of husbands
and the god's fixed stare.

4

It was a system:
we loved each other,
the war began on Vega,
we watched the hurtling lights,
and the silence drained us.

5

Out of spit and dust
we made two lovers
who set fire to the world.

from *Fence*

Song: *I Love You.*
Who are You?

◇　◇　◇

For several years in middle age I fell in love
   With celebrated women, Maria Callas and
Miss Monkey Business (from a local band),
   Then Dolly Parton. O Dolly, in the spirit of the flesh,

Dolly any woman met any place I'd ever been.
   And later in the evening of that night
I asked if she would shed
   That blond Aldebaran wig and the make-up, please,

Spike heels and that tightest
   Cowgirl sequined dress she wore,
Then the reins that held her breasts.
   And there in the mirror we beheld

The girl she'd lost along the way—
   She was so tiny I was taller
Than I'd ever been,
   And, *Sing for me*, I begged.

I'm any man met anywhere
   Who does not matter, and will not, ever.
She sang that song about lost love and bad men,
   And there was me, a bad, lost loveable man again,

Full of too much whiskey, tired
   Of ogling the beauties in the mirrors
Of the roadhouse bars. I'd lost my job,
   I'd lost our tickets out of here, become that man
Who stuttered, howled, wept,
   Fell down in the gravel parking lot, cursed,
Swallowed my tobacco, and said *I'm sorry, Ma'am,*
   And she said, to the bunch grass,

To the cows, *He's just a bad man*
   Gone good. Or maybe, *He's just mine.*
And took my arm and off we walked
   To charm the hollows of the glens

Where every rock and tree could be
   A member of the wedding of the rocks and trees.

from *Gulf Coast*

101

Dear Owl

◊   ◊   ◊

Dear Owl
you have big eyes

feathers that stick in all different directions
you wake up

your panties are funny
You hear

the sounds words make
as they plead for life

that's all that remains
of the language of language

O Owl
among leaves

what is this forest
of "letters," black light

of unintelligible suns
I cannot see

who I am
who you are

the difference between good and evil
the end of human desire

how to tell the truth
and why

Is this my life
Are you in it

from *jubilat*

Death Is Intended

◊   ◊   ◊

On Feb. 6, 67-year-old Guy Waterman—naturalist, outdoorsman,
devoted husband . . . decided to climb a New Hampshire mountain, lie
down on the cold stones and die overnight of exposure. "Death is intended"
he wrote.

—New York Times Book Review

. . . the melancholy beauty of giving it all up.
—Robert Hass

Isn't that what Eskimos did when they were old,
dragged themselves through a wilderness
of ice and up some mountain?
Then they could fall asleep forever,
their dark eyes speckled with falling snow—
not suicide exactly, but the opening
of a door so death could enter.
"Quit while you're ahead," my father told me
as I was feeding quarters into slot machines.
And that's what Waterman did, he quit
before infirmity could catch him, or other afflictions
whose breath he could already smell.
But I wanted more: a waterfall of coins
spilt on my lap, the raw electric charge
of money. I came away with nothing;
but I still want more, if only more chapters
in the family book I'm part of: I want
to read all the unfolding stories—each child
a mystery only time can solve.

Was it bravery or cowardice, what Waterman did,
or are those simply two sides of a coin,
like the coin some casual God might flip,
deciding who would live or die that day?
I'd rather flip the coin myself, but not at 67.
And not quite yet, I tell myself at 70, as spring
streams in over our suburban hills, enflaming
even the white New Hampshire mountains.

from *Shenandoah*

Dislocations:
Seven Scenarios

◇　◇　◇

1.

Still learning the word
"home" or what it could mean
                              say, to relinquish

a backdrop of japanese maples turning
color of rusted wheelbarrow bottom
where the dahlia tubers were thrown

You must go live in the city now
over the subway though not on
                              its grating

must endure the foreign music
of the block party

finger in useless anger
the dangling cords of the windowblind

2.

In a vast dystopic space the small things
multiply

when all the pills run out the pain
grows more general

flies find the many eyes
quarrels thicken then

                         weaken

tiny mandibles of rumor open and close
blame has a name that will not be spoken

you grasp or share a clot of food
according to your nature

                         or your strength

love's ferocity snarls
from under the drenched blanket's hood

3.

City and world: this infection drinks like a drinker
whatever it can

casual salutations first
little rivulets of thought

then wanting stronger stuff
sucks at the marrow of selves

the nurse's long knowledge of wounds
the rabbi's scroll of ethics
the young worker's defiance

only the solipsist seems intact
in her prewar building

4.

For recalcitrancy of attitude
the surgeon is transferred
to the V.A. hospital   where poverty
is the administrator
of necessity and her

orders don't necessarily
get obeyed
because
the government
is paying
and the
used to be
warriors
are patients

5.

Faces in the mesh: defiance or disdain
    remember Paul Nizan?
        You thought you were innocent if you said

"I love this woman and I want to live
    in accordance with my love."
        but you were beginning the revolution

maybe so, maybe not
    look at her now
        pale lips papery flesh

at your creased belly   wrinkled sac
    look at the scars
        reality's autographs

along your ribs across her haunches
look at the collarbone's reverberant line

    how in a body can defiance
        still embrace its likeness

6.

Not to get up and go back to the drafting table
where failure crouches accusing
like the math test you bluffed and flunked

so early on
not to drag into the window's
cruel and truthful light   your blunder
not to start over

but to turn your back, saying
all anyway is compromise
impotence and collusion
from here on I will be no part of it

is one way could you afford it

7.

Tonight someone will sleep in a stripped apartment
the last domestic traces, cup and towel
awaiting final disposal

—has ironed his shirt for travel
left an envelope for the cleaning woman
on the counter under the iron

internationalist turning toward home
three continents to cross   documents declarations
searches queues

and home no simple matter
of hearth or harbor
bleeding from internal wounds

he diagnosed   physician
without frontiers

from *Boston Review*

All the Ghosts

◊   ◊   ◊

Their dream decelerates our spinning planet
one millimeter-per-second per century
until they have matched velocity with us
and can stride into our lives and live again—

a matter of eons, nothing to them, so patient,
since the massed wish of all the dead
is only the slide of a hem across a floor,
or the difference on your face of milder air.

It is their fate, they murmur. It is anyway their way
to shun the theatrical or gothic gesture.
They would not rattle chains if chains could hold them.
It is the wind, so much stronger, that slams doors.

They are heard, if ever, in the dramas of your dreams
where you cannot tell still voices from your own,
intervening, if at all, in the neural substrate,
shunting a lone election *Maybe* or *Maybe not.*

Theirs are evasive and oblique persuasions,
stone by stream, for example, snows on outer planets,
undetected constants haunting physicists,
eddies where time runs sidelong or remembers.

Their delight is yielding, wind within the wind,
to faint velleities or fainter chances,
for they find among death's consolations, few enough,
the greatest is, to be mistaken for what happens.

When your eyes widen, they are surging to observe
the evening's trend to mauve, and all you have chosen
so slowly you are unaware of choosing.
And you may feel them feel, amused or touched

(history has not been long enough to decide which)
when your blunt patience emulates their own,
when you sense, like them, all fate might well be focused
in the exact glint of a right front hoof uplifted,

when you wait, as they must, for that crisis of precision
when it will make all the difference in the world
whether a particular petal's side-slipping fall
hushes the rim of a glass, or misses.

from *The Paris Review*

How I Became Impossible

◇ ◇ ◇

I was born shy, congenitally unable to do anything
profitable, to see anything in color, to love plums,
with a marked aversion to traveling around the room,
which is perfectly normal in infants.
Who wrote this? were my first words.
I did not like to be torched.
More snow fell than was able to melt,
I became green-eyed and in due time traveled
to other countries where I formed opinions
on hard, cold, shiny objects and soft, warm,
nappy things. Late in life I began to develop
a passion for persimmons and was absolutely delighted
when a postcard arrived for the recently departed.
I became recalcitrant, spending more and more time
with my rowboat. All my life I thought polar bears
and penguins grew up together playing side by side
on the ice, sharing the same vista, bits of blubber
and innocent lore. One day I read a scientific journal:
there are no penguins at one pole, no bears
on the other. These two, who were so long intimates
in my mind, began to drift apart, each on his own floe,
far out into the glacial seas. I realized I was becoming
impossible, more and more impossible,
and that one day it really would be true.

from *Court Green*

Home to Roost

◇   ◇   ◇

The chickens
are circling and
blotting out the
day. The sun is
bright, but the
chickens are in
the way. Yes,
the sky is dark
with chickens,
dense with them.
They turn and
then they turn
again. These
are the chickens
you let loose
one at a time
and small—
various breeds.
Now they have
come home
to roost—all
the same kind
at the same speed.

from *Poetry*

Media Effects

◊   ◊   ◊

advertising is Poetry with a small "p"
poetry is Advertising with a small "a"

advertising is Advertising with a small "a"
poetry is Poetry with a small "p"

movies are Film with a small "f"
music is Film with a small "m"

TV is poetry with a small screen
filled with big ads and tiny shows

poetry is TV with a non-economic ambition
TV is a poem that scoffs at prestige

movies are pretentious TV shows pretending to be poems
poems are movies for those who think advertising is the
      greatest art form

advertising is the favorite art form of most poets
this is why so many of them want to write for the movies

from *Insurance Magazine*

Costanza Bonarelli

◇   ◇   ◇

A bust that looks just-kissed,
from the blind intensity
of her gaze, to the somewhat swollen
parted lips, to the parting,
above her rumpled chemise,
of two soft breasts in his hands
lifted from stone, Bernini's

lover had been designed
to please—to have and hold
in his own eyes as forever
undone and to-be-done-to,
a melting readiness.
Oh the inconstant Costanza,
true-to-life but untrue!—

whose drawing power, coiled
as the heavy braid he pulled
behind her head, yet loose
as the involving tendrils
that tumbled to one side,
originated from
within a designing woman.

If either alone suffices
(love or art, that is)
to lead a man to believe
whole days can be best spent
lost in a woman's hair,

how could he not have wept
    at the upswept and downfallen

        tresses of one who was
    both singular ideal—
a thing he'd hacked from rock
    into his own landmark
        in portraiture, quintessence
of the sinuous baroque—
    and all too two-faced mistress?

    That she was capable
    of deception—this was fine,
one guesses: a frisson
    at first that she (the wife
        of his apprentice) gave
in private no resistance
    to a greater man's assistance.

        But now the great man's brother?
    His brother? When the rumor
reached him, Bernini sent
    a razor-bearing servant
        to do what must be done.
He wasn't going to kill her.
    No, but he'd leave a scar,

        a sort of *Kilroy was here*;
    he'd affix his stamp, he'd fix her
once and for all, for good—
    indeed, he'd have some thug
        or other slash her face,
her living flesh, with a tool
    not so unlike the one

        that he alone, the master,
    had been skilled enough to wield,
watching the marble yield
    to each sweet, painstaking stroke

of chisel against cheek
until, so real, she'd fairly
cried out for more.

from *The American Scholar*

The Grilled Cheese Sandwich

An Elusive Essential to Social Success

◇　◇　◇

1. On Acquiring a Social Position

A well-made grilled cheese sandwich can open a vista
leading to popularity and the possibilities
for "a good time."

2. On the Life of the Party

Where the perfect grilled cheese sandwich is
the successful party is also.

3. The Mark of a Social Climber

When you see a woman in silks and sables
speak to a grilled cheese sandwich as if it were dirt
you may be sure she hasn't come far
from the ground herself.

4. On Freshness

"Keep your hands on your own grilled cheese!"
might be the first chapter in any book
on etiquette.

5. ON COARSE LANGUAGE

Coarse slang is beside the mark but a good
grilled cheese sandwich cannot help but elicit
an enthusiastic "Right O!"

6. ON EXPRESSION

There should be a quality of protectiveness
in a man's expression when it falls on his grilled cheese
sandwich. As though so lovely a breath might break it.

7. ON DECENCY

The phrases devised to close a letter to a betrothed
are limited only by imagination
but do not belong in this or any other grilled cheese sandwich.

8. A NOTE TO THE GENTLEMAN

It would be presumptuous to tell any man how to prepare
his own grilled cheese sandwich when the answer is written
in his heart, his intellect, and his ardent civic pride.

from *Barrow Street* and *Good Foot*

Moscow

◇　◊　◇

For a while I was alone,
so I dated whoever's work I was reading,
but the relationships always ended badly.
I wasn't smart enough for Wayne,
I wasn't caustic enough for David,
Kevin & I were doing well,
but then I met his real boyfriend,
and it turns out I'm not his type.
Sometimes I broke it off.
Jean got to be too depressing.
Fyoder was a bad provider.
After Franz, I started dating myself,
and that was nice. Of course, then I met you
and I had to stop being the man in my life.
I miss me sometimes, but we'll always have Moscow.

from *Shankpainter*

Hate Poem

◊ ◊ ◊

I hate you. Truly I do.
Everything about me hates everything about you.
The flick of my wrist hates you.
The way I hold my pencil hates you.
The sound made by my tiniest bones were they trapped in the jaws of a moray
     eel hates you.
Each corpuscle singing in its capillary hates you.

Look out! Fore! I hate you.

The little blue-green speck of sock lint I'm trying to dig from under my third
     toenail, left foot, hates you.
The history of this keychain hates you.
My sigh in the background as you pick out the cashews hates you.
The goldfish of my genius hates you.
My aorta hates you. Also my ancestors.

A closed window is both a closed window and an obvious symbol of how I
     hate you.

My voice curt as a hairshirt: hate.
My hesitation when you invite me for a drive: hate.
My pleasant "good morning": hate.
You know how when I'm sleepy I nuzzle my head under your arm? Hate.
The whites of my target-eyes articulate hate. My wit practices it.
My breasts relaxing in their holster from morning till night hate you.
Layers of hate, a parfait.
Hours after our last row, brandishing the sharp glee of hate,
I dissect you cell by cell, so that I may hate each one individually and at leisure.

My lungs, duplicitous twins, expand with the utter validity of my hate, which
can never have enough of you,
Breathlessly, like two idealists in a broken submarine.

from *Pleiades*

CHARLES SIMIC

Sunlight

◇　◇　◇

As if you had a message for me . . .
Tell me about the grains of dust
On my night table?
Are any one of them worth your trouble?

Your burglaries leave no thumbprint
Mine, too, are silent.
I do my best imagining at night,
And you do yours with the help of shadows.

Like actors rehearsing a play,
The dark ones withdrew
Into remote corners of the room.
The rest of us sat in expectation
Of your burning oratory.

If you did say something, I'm none the wiser.
The breakfast finished,
The coffee dregs were unenlightening.
Like a lion cage at feeding time,
The floor at my feet turned red.

from *New England Review*

LOUIS SIMPSON

An Impasse

◇　◇　◇

Jacques writes from Paris,
"What are the latest news?"

I have told him, time
and time again, "What are"

is not English, "news"
is not plural, "news"

is a singular term,
as in "The news is good."

He replies, "Though 'The news'
may be singular in America,

it is not so in France.
Les nouvelles is a plural term.

To say, 'The news is good'
in France would be bad grammar,

and absurd, which is worse.
On the other hand, 'What are

the news?' makes perfect sense."

from *The Hudson Review*

W. D. SNODGRASS

For Hughes Cuenod
—in his 100th year

◇　　◇　　◇

Midway along our road sometimes a voice
Sounds, prohibiting all heldenblustering choices
　　Of timbre, overtones or fashions;
Fifty years back, when I first heard you sing
I thought: "The poems I've written lack for nothing
　　But such clarity, such passion."

With Nadia Boulanger when young, you went
Touring through languages and continents,
　　Collegia, festivals and venues;
To countertenor from youth's baritone,
You made each form, period and style your own,
　　Tasting your way down this art's menu.

From Frescobaldi, Couperin, Monteverdi,
To Neidhardt, Bach, Schutz' Sacred Concerti
　　Then Fauré, Debussy, Auric;
Di Lasso to "A Lover and His Lass,"
Josquin to Stravinsky's *Rake's Progress*.
　　Machaut's Mass to Coward's *Bitter Sweet*.

With an untroubled, easy grace and verve,
You'd fill in for a friend whose wrenched-up nerves
　　Failed, sang through 60 years unchanged
By travel, time or untold cigarettes.
At 85, you called your debut at the Met
　　"A little bonbon after lunch."

"How could I lose my voice," you were known to banter;
"I never had one"—just a dry, white unmannered
   Mask tone with the bel canto breathing
That carried your song's deep impulse truly
From mouth to nerve ends like a fine, rich Pouilly.
   Why not just say: one voice for all seasons.

from *The New Criterion* and *Early Music America*

GARY SNYDER

Waiting for a Ride

◊   ◊   ◊

Standing at the baggage, passing time:
Austin, Texas, airport—my ride hasn't come yet.
My former wife is making Web sites from her home,
one son's seldom seen,
the other one and his wife have a boy and girl of their own.
My wife and stepdaughter are spending weekdays in town
so she can get to high school.
My mother, ninety-six, still lives alone and she's in town, too,
always gets her sanity back just barely in time.
My former former wife has become a unique poet;
most of my work,
such as it is, is done.
Full moon was October 2nd this year,
I ate a mooncake, slept out on the deck,
white light beaming through the black boughs of the pine,
owl hoots and rattling antlers,
Castor and Pollux rising strong—
it's good to know that the polestar drifts!
That even our present night sky slips away,
not that I'll see it.
Or maybe I will, much later,
some far time walking the spirit path in the sky,
that long walk of spirits—where you fall right back into the
"narrow painful passageway of the Bardo"
squeeze your little skull
and there you are again

waiting for your ride

from *The New Yorker*

Twenty Questions

◊   ◊   ◊

Who wrote *Heart of Darkness*? And what's the name
Of Dale Evans's horse? Why did thieves steal
Charlie Chaplin's corpse? Can you explain
Hieroglyphs in shells? How do you feel?
How many grains of (popcorn, rice, sand) fill
This container? Why did they auction off
Maria Callas's underwear? Would you like a pill?
Do you feel tired, perhaps? Is that bed soft?
Can you remember your parents' wedding date?
Your own? Like a glass of milk? Some champagne?
How many rhymes in a sonnet? Something you ate?
Who invented Bacos? Think it will rain?
Lie back now. Shall I bring you some chips?
What's the answer? It's rising to your lips.

from *POOL*

End of the Day on Second

◊   ◊   ◊

Her husband, traveling for his company, is rarely home.
Alone, she keeps herself to herself except for the stores.

Once past their revolving doors those mouse-gray webs
of thought that hang around her head like crape soon

lose their grayness; give way to garlands of things, new
things, needed things. She is quick of step, clear of eye,

purposeful. Seven floors of exhilaration await her.
Escalator bound, she hardly pauses to touch a faux-fur

something whish, like all else blazing in its newness urges
invitation from every counter, every aisle: "Touch me,

open me, feel me, turn me over, unzip me, try me on,
read my label, my price-tag, touch me, oh touch me. . . ."

Finally, on second, in bras. Bras swarming everywhere,
giant pink moths at rest, empty cups clamoring,

"Fill me." It's late. Shoppers have left, yet there's time
to try a bra. Emerging from the booth, she stands, only

half dressed and head down, in aisle five, a bra hanging
from her hand. A floorwalker approaches. "May I help you?"

She doesn't look up, murmurs, "My husband is away."
At this, the kindly floorwalker takes her in his arms, her

face hidden on his shoulder. They stand, unmoving,
among the mothy bras which might at any moment rise

in a cloud and leave them, as I am leaving them now,
in their frozen pose, their endless closing time.

from *The Antioch Review*

The Swing

◇   ◇   ◇

"Where do we go from here?" I said to Dawn. "We found the little aban-
doned church. We passed the giant cairn of stones. We crossed the
brook with its bridge of rope. We climbed up and down the mountain
with its laurel in bloom. And now we're standing in a field of clover
under a blue sky with some huge, billowy clouds wafting over us. I don't
feel lost, but I have no idea where we are." Dawn smiled at me. "We're
visiting my childhood," she said. "I grew up in this field. See that
sycamore over there. My daddy made me a swing from that very branch.
My sisters and I played every kind of game that children play right
here in this field. In the summers, mama would call us to dinner and
we'd hide behind those big boulders. The house we lived in was over
there, at the edge of the forest. It burned down when I was twelve. And
that's when we moved to town. Nothing was ever the same again.
Daddy died a couple of years later, and mama kind of gave up on us girls.
The town was always strange to me. I felt like some kind of caged up wild
animal." "I never knew any of this about you, Dawn," I said. "Why did
you never tell me until now?" "After we left I never went back until today.
My childhood was literally burnt to the ground, my beautiful childhood,
and I never wanted to see it again. And now here we are, and I'm telling
you about it, and I'm torn right down the middle between sadness and
happiness." I could always tell when Dawn was beginning to believe one
of her little fantasies. She shrunk into herself and wouldn't look me in
the eye. So I said, "Let's get the hell out of here before it rains." I
grabbed her by the arm and started running into the forest. The forest
was quickly swallowing us up. This is what we do on weekends. We try
to find a happy childhood for Dawn, but they always turn ugly. She
insists on that. I had liked the part about her daddy making her a swing

on the sycamore, but she just couldn't leave it alone. She had to burn down the house.

from *New American Writing*

Marijuana

◇ ◇ ◇

Stoned by noon, I'd take the trail
that runs along the X River
in the State of Y, summer of '69,
crows' black ruckus overhead.
I'd wade through the ferns' sound
of vanishing to the almost-invisible ledge,
stark basin canted out to the southwest:
sheltered, good drainage,
full sun, remote, state land.
You could smell the blacker, foreign green
from a long way off when it rained,
incense-grade floral, the ripening spoils,
then pang of wood smoke,
antiseptic pitch and balsam,
scents cut like initials in a beech,
then cold that kills the world for a while,
puts it under, then wakes it up
again in spring when it's still tired.
I woke from its anesthesia
wanting the tight buds of my loneliness
to swell and split, not die in waiting.
It was why I rushed through everything,
why I tore away at the perpetual gauze
between me and the stinging world,
its starlight and resins,
new muscle married to smoke and tar,
just wedding the world for a while.
About to divorce it, too,
to marry some other smoke and tar.

On snowshoes in falling snow,
we lugged peat, manure,
and greensand a mile up there.
Alfalfa meal, spent hops.
The clones bronzed, hairy and sticky,
and a week before frost we'd slice
the dirt around them with a bread knife,
which gave the dope
a little extra turpentine.
Weed, reefer, smoke—
it was one of life's perfumes.
Sometimes its flower opens
on a city street, gray petals,
phantom musk dispersing.
The other day I caught myself
checking the matches to see
if all the dead ones faced backwards.
They did. It's an old habit,
a watchfulness over disorder,
an anxiety keeping its distance
like a feral dog that won't touch
anything kindness touched.

Sleeping out on the high ledges
on a bed of blueberries dwarfed
by wind and springy beneath the blankets,
we'd watch for meteors and talk till dawn,
gazing toward the pinnacle in the distance,
pyramid to the everlasting glory
of Never Enough, not far below us
in his tomb, asleep in the granite chill
with the bones of his faithful animals.

Could this be the pinnacle?
To be slumming back there
buoyant on the same old
wave just breaking,
now the wave of words, the liftoff?
I'm still cracking open the robin's egg
to see the yellow heart, the glue.

A pinnacle is a fulcrum,
a scale. And now that it's tipped,
I can look back through the ghost
of self-consciousness to its embryo,
first the tomboy,
then the chick in a deerskin skirt,
the first breaking of the spirit,
the heart's deflowerment.

Caw, caw, a crow wants to nip
the memory in the bud,
the ember of the mind
as it was before it tasted
the dark meat of the world.
But I can call it back—
the match's sulfur spurt,
its petals of carbon and tar,
a flash of mind, a memory:
how after each deflowerment,
I became the flower.

from *The Yale Review*

For a Man Who Wrote CUNT on a Motel Bathroom Mirror

◊   ◊   ◊

You thought she was asleep. You were afraid
To hear what she'd call *you*
If you said it out loud as a parting shot at the door,
So you took the sneaky way out
And used her own lipstick against her, against the mirror
Where you felt certain she'd look no later than dawn,
But would find, instead of herself
In there again behind glass, your blunt reflection,
Your last word on the subject.

But I'm here to tell you she was wide-awake.
Behind her eyelids she followed every move
Of yours, the jingle of small change
When you finally found your pants, the smallest squeak
Of your run-down heels in the bathroom,
The soft click of the latch.

She let out the breath she'd been holding and keeping
To herself, took a quick shower, considered
The small end of your vocabulary,
And taxied home. She didn't bother
Erasing your word, but passed it on
As a kind of tip to the maid, who wouldn't clean up

After you either, but left it to the imagination
Of another transient facing a cold morning,
Thinking of you and passing the word along.

from *Hanging Loose*

From the Notebooks of Anne Verveine, VII

◊ ◊ ◊

Distance was the house in which I welcomed you.
But it was in the river
that we became cadence, there where the current braided

together again, after the stone bridge stanchion parted the stream.
It was to last only as long as the beauty lasted.
Do you believe in the soul?

Words from the void, wet and mewling.
Where we walked on the mountain, water
poured around us, surged up from springs, seethed.

down in rivulets, rocky streams, and one long blinding cascade:
your kisses were an *eau-de-vie* and as bitter.
I am poured out like water.

Distance is feminine in French.
I held a knife to a man's throat and let him bleed quietly into a cup.
What does "us" mean?

Coiled serpentine headdress of Leonardo's woman:
you wanted her. I wanted you.
Chill sunlight flexing itself on the city river

gave me the emptiness I needed
to write these instructions: Sorrow
is a liqueur. Drink deep. We will all be consumed.

from *The New Yorker* and *Pleine Marge*

Ballad of the Subcontractor

◇ ◇ ◇

During his senior year, Francis won every blue ribbon
Debate. *Every debate, Francis?* "Yes,
Yes, I won them
All," he answered with no false modesty and no true
Modesty, either. Our Francis argued the death penalty fifty

Times that year. He was like a star quarterback but
Smaller, brighter. Odd to think of it,
Now that the workers who deserted are finally
Caught, I mean. We threw them in the lift, debated
Knocking them around
A bit. Their manifold arguments

Will accentuate those you already
Have. The cranes broke loose, they said. *Not likely.*
They lost our papers, hammers flew over the edge. Pneumatic
Drills advised them to do as they were told
In the old country. Francis liked to open each debate with

A rhetorical question. "Imagine, for a minute," he would say,
"That you are on death row." Closing his eyes, Francis
Shivered. It was his best
Debate; he won both sides over,
And over. He'd bend and sway; clasp his hands. I can't
Recall his ever giving me a cigarette for my smoking

Pleasure. The electricians who cursed us were finally
Sorry. During my junior year, Francis led
The team to a championship and carried a gold-plated

Trophy home. His role
Complemented mine. I won nothing back
In the day. Francis took everything and then

Some. Judges met to welcome
A new champion who
Understood the industrial and ritual uses of
Metal. The industrial uses of steel as building fabric, exoskeleton,
Are many, but the damage
Was done. Since then I've been altogether too
Busy, working overtime, really, to thank him, but events have borne out my
Fears and
Predictions. *You break a strike, you pay for it*
In spades, in the blocked road. In spite

Of the many arguments
Offered by those in favor of unions, I have
No opinion. In one
Corner a pile of bricks, in another
A jacket of Copper. Spatial order, but also, chronological
In that the bricks came first and the
Copper went up last with wired bits of glass so
That the foam of the capitol illuminates

The sun-blocked day and night.
This is my part in the skyline
Renovation project, brought to
You by someone or other, *those mugs*, money
Swindlers, fat cats, pocket shimmers, someone, I would
Guess, like that windbag Francis.

from *Notre Dame Review*

from "The Maud Project"

◊   ◊   ◊

JUDAS PRIEST

You can't sit there and tell me anything you've said here is true.

Lace our shut eyes shut.

Don't you ping my machine. Young lady.

SHE'S A PILL

Oh, dangling long sleeves in the Mercurochrome. Parking
her punch on her knees.

I'm not a joiner.

In the night, a visitation, small as a thumb,
enters the sealed house and ascends.

Mother wouldn't have stood for *that* long. Drippy-drooping
around on heels. Leaving the blue cheese out.

BUSIER THAN A CRANBERRY BOG MERCHANT

Serif or sanserif; the latter will give you a cleaner line, more
legible sign. Directionals made a strong sixty cent stripe, I could
have told you that. Replenish. Replenish my glass. The crane in the
cocktail onion jar. Earth Shoes giving out.

It's the Time Machine's tunnel, and my own wavery voice waving back
from the walls of its chute's what I hear. But her own's near my ear.

Oh, the bone's the best part. Em ess. Mouth shut.

A GOOD EGG

But that was mother. I knew I looked good when she said, "Cut
your lip?" Ray, the dog got out. You'll have to pick off the burs.

Headlong onto the grass, a crow and its silken down
drops, black bomb. Child on a bird's back streams like a kite.

She was sharp as a tack, always was. Can you take the hint?

from *Salt*

RICHARD WILBUR

Some Words Inside of Words

(for children and others)

◇　◇　◇

The *roc*'s a huge, bold, hungry bird who's able
To eat an elephant. (So says the fable.)
No farmer likes to see one feasting cockily
Right in the middle of his field of *broccoli*.

At heart, *ambassadors* are always *sad*.
Why? Because world affairs are always bad,
So that they're always having to express
"Regret," and "grave concern," and "deep distress."

The *barnacle* is found in salty seas,
Clinging to rocks in crusty colonies;
And salt, which chemists call $NaCl$,
Is found inside the barnacle as well.

What could be sillier than for a *cow*
To try to cross the ocean in a *scow*?
With such a captain, to my way of thinking,
The wretched vessel would be sure of sinking!
No one should be entrusted with a rudder
Who has two horns and four hooves and an udder.

If a *carp* is in your *carport*, go find out
Whether the living room is full of trout
And eels and salamanders, and if there's
A snapping turtle paddling up the stairs.

If that's what's going on, your house (beyond
A doubt) is at the bottom of a pond.

Some snakes are nice to handle, but an *asp*
Is not the kind to take within your *grasp.*
That is what Cleopatra did, I fear,
And, as you know, she is no longer here.

from *The Atlantic Monthly*

Bareback Pantoum

◇　◇　◇

One night, bareback and young, we rode through the woods
and the woods were on fire—
two borrowed horses, two local boys
whose waists we clung to, my sister and I,

and the woods were on fire—
the pounding of hooves and the smell of smoke and the sharp sweat of boys
whose waists we clung to, my sister and I,
as we rode toward flame with the sky in our mouths—

the pounding of hooves and the smell of smoke and the sharp sweat of boys
and the heart saying: *mine*
as we rode toward flame with the sky in our mouths—
the trees turning gold, then crimson, white

and the heart saying: *mine*
of the wild, bright world;
the trees turning gold, then crimson, white
as they burned in the darkness, and we were girls

of the wild, bright world
of the woods near our house—we could turn, see the lights
as they burned in the darkness, and we were girls
so we rode just to ride

through the woods near our house—we could turn, see the lights—
and the horses would carry us, carry us home
so we rode just to ride,
my sister and I, just to be close to the danger of love

and the horses would carry us, carry us home
—two borrowed horses, two local boys,
my sister and I—just to be close to that danger, desire—
one night, bareback and young, we rode through the woods.

from *New Letters*

A Short History of My Life

◇   ◇   ◇

Unlike Lao-tzu, conceived of a shooting star, it is said,
And carried inside his mother's womb
For 62 years, and born, it's said once again, with white hair,
I was born on a Sunday morning,
                                untouched by the heavens,
Some hair, no teeth, the shadows of twilight in my heart,
And a long way from the way.
Shiloh, the Civil War battleground, was just next door,
The Tennessee River soft shift at my head and feet.
The dun-colored buffalo, the sands of the desert,
Gatekeeper and characters
                        were dragon years from then.

Like Dionysus, I was born for a second time.
From the flesh of Italy's left thigh, I emerged one January
Into a different world.
                        It made a lot of sense,
Hidden away, as I had been, for almost a life.
And I entered it open-eyed, the wind in my ears,
The slake of honey and slow wine awake on my tongue.
Three years I stood in S. Zeno's doors,
                        and took, more Rome than Rome,
Whatever was offered me.
The snows of the Dolomites advanced to my footfalls.
The lemons of Lago di Garda fell to my hands.

Fast-forward some forty-five years,
                                and a third postpartum blue.
But where, as the poet asked, will you find it in history?

Alluding to something else.
Nowhere but here, my one and only, nowhere but here.
My ears and my sick senses seem pure with the sound of water.
I'm back, and it's lilac time,
The creeks running eastward unseen through the dank morning,
Beginning of June. No light on leaf,
No wind in the evergreens, no bow in the still-blond grasses.
The world in its dark grace.
                    I have tried to record it.

                    from *The New Yorker*

A Big Ball of Foil in
a Small New York Apartment

◊   ◊   ◊

"It will flame out . . ."
—Hopkins

It began with a single sheet, leftover from his lunch.
His unthinking palm had reached out to it, slapped down
on the center of it, and begun gathering and compacting it
until soon he had a small firm ball in his fist.
He squeezed the ball tightly, as tightly as he could.
Now the ball was, if not as firm as possible,
at least as firm as he could easily make it,
and he took from this the small satisfaction it offered.
It felt good. In fact, as his fingers opened out
into their individual selves again, he saw the ball
in his slightly dented palm, as in a nest,
it occurred to him that there were many good things
to be felt about this ball: its crinkled surface
would keep it from rolling off at the slightest tilt;
it wouldn't come undone like balled-up paper can;
and that it was all crumpled foil, 100% through
seemed to contain a kind of meaning,
(though truly what it was he wasn't sure). . . .
It was then he had an idea. Like light on water
it danced across his thinking, absorbing his attention.
He would add to this ball, add to it until it was huge;
he wouldn't throw it out as he had so many others.
And how many had he thrown out? The unknowable number

(exaggerated for effect) jostled him all over, like nerves,
for you see, he had begun to imagine the ball quite large,
and the thought that the foil in his little ball
might have existed as a nearly flat sheet on the surface
of an already enormous ball boggled him.
But he knew it wasn't good to think like that,
and he snapped quickly to, nodding and determined.
He would grow the ball from this point forward.
Foil was everywhere. It wouldn't be hard.
So from that day on as he walked the streets,
although he let his thoughts drift as they wished,
(seeing, for instance, the sun seep free from behind a cloud
he'd think, in the brief spell before it disappeared behind another,
of hundreds of suddenly pleased sunbathers in rows on a beach;
he'd think of sweaty red-faced men carrying heavy wooden crates)
he kept his sights always alive to the prospect
of foil's particular glint. When he'd see a stranded sheet
in a corner garbage can or on a restaurant table,
he'd glance sharply about, to see if anyone was watching him,
slyly pocket it, then shuffle off at a quickened pace.
Early on, it bothered him, and he'd have to reassure himself:
"No one is looking; no one cares; this city is full
of stranger things than a man collecting foil."
Over time, he began to believe this truth, or rather,
the shame he couldn't help but feel was overcome.
For there was nothing much better than walking about,
as twilight approached, with a good take bulging his pockets.
It was a feeling not unlike knowing a wonderful secret,
or being, perhaps, a bottle with a message in it.
However, at such bright excited times,
much like an island surfacing in a drought-sucked stream,
the ball as he wished it could be, huge and shining
and exactly round, would give rise in his mind.
It was awesome and beautiful, but not a good thing,
and he tried to keep it happening, to hide it away,
like that heart under the floorboards in the Poe story
that had terrified him as a child. For his own ball
when he'd return home, became so inadequate then,
so silly and lopsided and small. Emptying his pockets,
smoothing the foil with a rolling pin (his system),

he'd murmur sound, sobering sayings to himself like:
"nothing turns out the way you thought it would,"
and "it'll take years." But time was one thing he had,
and the progress, albeit slow, was steady.
As the months went by, the ball grew. It grew and grew.
It grew until it had to be moved from the oven,
where he'd kept it to save space, into the open, onto the floor.
It grew until it couldn't fit through the window or the door.
It grew until furniture had to be moved, first
to new places in his apartment, then out onto the street.
It was then he knew the ball was there to stay. . . .
But though he'd been one that had wanted the ball,
often he felt ambivalently, and this ambivalence grew too.
Why was he doing what he was?
Why was he filling his apartment, his mind, with foil?
It was not something he preferred to wonder about,
and he tried hard to keep the wondering out, to ignore it
as one might a dog that's scratching at a door.
But ridiculous as he acknowledged the ball to be,
if you were to have caught him at the right moment,
you would have seen how he loved it.
Certain nights, after he'd measured it in all directions,
(by setting up a spotlight and measuring the shadows)
then peeled and patched it to preserve its roundness,
(the ball's defining, so most important quality)
he'd step away (as away as he could),
and those narrowed-up, fault-inventing eyes of his
would soften into something like appreciation.
Spot-lit like that, the ball gave back a cool, fragile light
much as he'd heard the earth did when seen by astronauts,
and he'd feel suddenly lucky to be where he was,
standing in the strange and silvery shine. Coming to,
he'd often find an inch of ash on his cigarette. . . .
So it was kind of sad then, that this ball should end,
should stop growing, even though all along
it'd been what he'd been working towards.
He didn't know what he was going to do.
Would he still see a city speckled with foil?
Or would what once was treasure dull
to trash again? There was no way to predict.

The night he was done, the night the ball
nudged up against his ceiling and his walls
(a coincidence so long foreseen it had lost its luster)
he pressed his teeth deep into its surface, as a signature,
leaned his confused body against it, closed his eyes,
and, listening to the cars pass, wept a little bit.

August 11–14, 2003

from *New York Quarterly*

Black Cat Blues

◇   ◇   ◇

I showed up for jury duty—
turns out the one on trial was me.

Paid me for my time & still
I couldn't make bail.

Judge that showed up
was my ex-wife.

Now that was some
hard time.

She sentenced me
to remarry.

I chose firing squad instead.
Wouldn't you know it—

Plenty of volunteers
to take the first shot

But no one wanted to spring
for the bullets.

Governor commuted my sentence to life
in a cell more comfortable

Than this here skin
I been living in.

from *Virginia Quarterly Review*

CONTRIBUTORS'
NOTES AND
COMMENTS

A. R. AMMONS was born outside Whiteville, North Carolina, in 1926. He started writing poetry aboard a U.S. Navy destroyer escort in the South Pacific. After completing service in World War II, he attended Wake Forest University. He went on to work as an executive in his father-in-law's biological glass company before he began teaching at Cornell University in 1964. Ammons wrote nearly thirty books of poetry, many published by W. W. Norton, including *Glare* (1997); *Garbage* (1993), which won the National Book Award and the Library of Congress's Rebekah Johnson Bobbitt National Prize for Poetry; *A Coast of Trees* (1981), which received the National Book Critics Circle Award for Poetry; *Sphere* (1974), which received the Bollingen Prize; and *Collected Poems 1951–1971* (1972), which won the National Book Award. He lived in Ithaca, New York, where he was Goldwin Smith Professor of Poetry at Cornell University until his retirement in 1998. He was the guest editor of *The Best American Poetry 1994*. Ammons died on February 25, 2001.

"In View of the Fact" appeared in a special all-Ammons issue of *Epoch*, edited by Roger Gilbert, which contained poems, journals, and letters from (and to) the late poet. The poems were accompanied by commentary from leading critics and friends. Helen Vendler characterized "In View of the Fact" as "a self-elegy, but it is about dying as one of a generation—'the people of my time.'" She notes that "the poem skirts sentimentality, but is saved by its modals: the sun 'may' shine, we will 'as we must' bequeath the past to others, and love 'can' (but it may not necessarily) grow. Hope and necessity and possibility, in the stoic candor of those about to die, replace the former self-solacing illusions of prophecy and will. In this moving lament for the lost, ego and effacement meet in the anteroom of death."

JOHN ASHBERY was born in Rochester, New York, in 1927. He is the author of more than twenty books of poetry, including *Self-Portrait in a*

Convex Mirror, which won the Pulitzer Prize in 1976, and *Where Shall I Wander* (Ecco Press/Carcanet, 2005). A Harvard alumnus, he gave that university's Norton Lectures on Thomas Lovell Beddoes, John Clare, Laura Riding, Raymond Roussel, David Schubert, and John Wheelwright. Ashbery's *Selected Prose*, edited by Eugene Richie, was published in 2004 by the University of Michigan Press in its Poets on Poetry series and by Carcanet in the United Kingdom. Ashbery was guest editor of the inaugural volume of *The Best American Poetry* in 1988. Since 1990 he has been the Charles P. Stevenson, Jr., Professor of Languages and Literature at Bard College. He divides his time between Hudson, New York, and New York City.

MAUREEN BLOOMFIELD was born in Cleveland, Ohio, on July 4, 1950. Because she had severe asthma, her family moved to St. Petersburg Beach, Florida, where she grew up. Her collection of poems, *Error and Angels*, appeared in 1997 (University of South Carolina Press). She has written on contemporary art for *Artforum* and *ARTnews*. Formerly a senior editor of *The Artist's Magazine*, she now edits *The Pastel Journal*. She lives in Cincinnati, Ohio, with her husband, James Cummins, and their two daughters.

Bloomfield writes: "The actual *Catholic Encyclopedia* defies description. My 'Catholic Encyclopedia' is almost a found poem."

CATHERINE BOWMAN was born in El Paso, Texas, in 1957. She lives in Bloomington, Indiana, and teaches at Indiana University. She is the author of *1-800-HOT-RIBS* (Gibbs Smith, 1993) and *Rock Farm* (Gibbs Smith, 1996). She edited *Word of Mouth: Poems Featured on NPR's All Things Considered* (Vintage, 2003). *One Thousand Lines*, her new collection of poems, is forthcoming from Four Way Books in 2006.

Of "I Want to Be Your Shoebox," Bowman writes: "One midsummer afternoon, listening to a CD called *Classic Blues* (Smithsonian Folkways Recordings), annotated and compiled by Barry Lee Pearson, I came across this paragraph by Pearson in the liner notes: 'Moreover, anyone looking at early Folkways song transcriptions can see how hard it was for New Yorkers to piece together song lyrics. Not only did they find the dialect formidable, but they seldom knew much about context. One well-meaning transcriber heard Memphis Minnie's classic line 'I want to be your chauffeur' as 'I want to be your shoebox.'" This became the inspiration, title, and epigraph for my poem. I was reading also a book called *Reading Lyrics* at the time. I remember Memphis Minnie's famous line as 'won't you be my chauffeur,' not 'I want to be your chauffeur,' but maybe I'm confusing one song for another.

"Every April in southern Indiana, where I live, old-timers and locals harvest rare and delicious morels from top-secret spots, usually from some forsaken apple orchard or the ruins of dying black elms. What is a floating dock diary? A floating dock diary is an anchored wooden raft in the middle of a beautiful lake, probably in Vermont or upstate New York, that you can swim out to in July and have homemade ice cream. It was fun to write these and hard to stop, a kind of guilty pleasure."

STEPHANIE BROWN was born in Pasadena, California, in 1961, and grew up in Newport Beach. She earned degrees from Boston University, the University of Iowa, and the University of California at Berkeley. She is the author of *Allegory of the Supermarket* (University of Georgia Press, 1999), and her poems and essays have appeared in many recent anthologies, including *The Grand Permission: New Writing on Poetics and Motherhood* (Wesleyan University Press, 2003) and *Great American Prose Poems: From Poe to the Present* (Scribner, 2003). She has primarily made her living as a public librarian since 1989. She lives with her family in San Clemente, California.

Of "Roommates: Noblesse Oblige, *Sprezzatura*, and Gin Lane," Brown writes: "I was once in a car for several hours, and as we drove on a winding road through a snowy and deserted landscape, one person in the car talked without stopping, bragging about her friends, acquaintances, and relatives, and she used two phrases to describe these people: '*enor*mously gifted' and '*exceed*ingly bright.' These phrases have come to mind occasionally during the twenty years since I first heard them. The first line of this poem, containing these phrases, came into my mind one morning last year as I was standing in my kitchen about to drink my morning cup of coffee. The opening line got me to think back to twenty years ago, when, earnest *arriviste* that I was, I was musing a lot about concepts like *sprezzatura*. The poem's details and distinctions about class and caste in American society I leave to the reader to discover; I must have happened upon them by blundering mistake, as I am truly not gifted or brilliant enough to make sense of them, hailing, as I do, from Southern California."

CHARLES BUKOWSKI was born in Andernach, Germany, in 1920, the only child of an American soldier and a German mother. At the age of three, he came with his family to the United States and grew up in Los

Angeles. He attended Los Angeles City College from 1939 to 1941, then left school and moved to New York City to become a writer. He gave up writing in 1946 when he began a ten-year stint of heavy drinking. After he developed a bleeding ulcer, he decided to take up writing again. He worked a wide range of jobs to support his writing, including mail carrier and postal clerk, dishwasher, guard, elevator operator, gas station attendant, stock boy, warehouse worker, and shipping clerk. His first story appeared when he was twenty-four and he began writing poetry at the age of thirty-five. He wrote, he once said, for "the defeated, the demented, and the damned." His first book of poetry was published in 1959; he went on to publish more than forty-five books of poetry and prose, including *The Last Night of the Earth Poems* (Black Sparrow Press, 1992), *Post Office* (Black Sparrow, 1980), and *Sifting Through the Madness for the Word, the Line, the Way* (Ecco, 2003). He died of leukemia in 1994.

ELENA KARINA BYRNE was born in Los Angeles, California, in 1959, and was educated at Sarah Lawrence College. She runs the reading series for University of Southern California's Doheny Memorial Library, and the Ruskin Art Club series with Red Hen Press. She is also coeditor of *The Los Angeles Literary Review* for 2004–5. *The Flammable Bird* (2002), her first book of poems, is available from Zoo Press. She has just completed another, *MASQUE*, and is working on a collection of essays on poetry and contemporary culture: *Poetry and Insignificance.*

Byrne writes: "'Irregular Masks' is one of the few poems in my new manuscript, *MASQUE*, in which the speaker addresses a generalized group. Because the poems are layered personae (specific and abstract), nearly all the poems simultaneously address the self and the epigraph so that the voice is also engendered by wild occurrence. I like to think of the process of the poem unfolding from the pronoun 'they,' to a dissolving— like the snowflake—'you.' Language, in all its lack of uniformity, mimics what we are; therefore we are constantly conjugating ourselves with an unpredictable exercise of speech. It's as if one beats one's head against the green wall of waves until the fish of the unconscious fly out."

VICTORIA CHANG was born in Detroit, Michigan, in 1970. She holds degrees from the University of Michigan, Harvard, and Stanford. *Circle,* her first book of poetry, won the Crab Orchard Review Open Competition and was published by Southern Illinois University Press in 2005. She is the editor of an anthology entitled *Asian American Poetry: The Next*

Generation (University of Illinois Press, 2004). She attended the low-residency graduate writing program at Warren Wilson College. She works as a researcher at the Stanford Graduate School of Business and owns her own consulting business. She resides in Los Angeles and San Diego.

Chang writes: "The fact that I have the most common surname in the world and possess the same full name as several people in the United States spurred me to write 'Seven Changs.' I was also thinking of my sister's friend, a brilliant man with a unique identity, who was named Bruce Lee, and at whom, therefore, people made kung-fu noises and shadowboxing motions everywhere he went.

"In the poem, I allowed words to spring from prior words through slant rhyme, consonance, and assonance. The poem is stitched together through language that morphs slightly as the poem progresses: 'lamps' and 'limp,' 'opal' and 'Oracle,' 'Chang' and 'Changed,' 'seashore' and 'Shared.'"

SHANNA COMPTON was born in Temple, Texas, in 1970. She attended the University of Texas at Austin and the graduate writing program at the New School in New York City. She is the associate publisher of Soft Skull Press in Brooklyn. Her first poetry collection, *Down Spooky*, won the Winnow Press Open Poetry Award and is forthcoming this fall. She is the editor of the video-game anthology *Gamers: Writers, Artists & Programmers on the Pleasures of Pixels* (Soft Skull, 2004), and maintains a poetry blog at www.shannacompton.com/blog.html.

Of "To Jacques Pépin," Compton writes: "This poem is a love letter to chef Jacques Pépin. I've always enjoyed watching him at work—particularly with Julia Child—on the cooking shows he's done over the years, and his book *Jacques Pépin's Complete Techniques* is a well-thumbed favorite in my culinary library. At the time I wrote this poem, I was feeling pangs of jealousy provoked by his daughter, Claudine, who appeared with him in *Cooking with Claudine* and *Encore with Claudine*. Silly, I know; but her role in those shows is to play 'clueless in the kitchen,' so in this poem I try to show her up. I imagine myself to be a better cook and a better daughter, plus two things Claudine couldn't be: lover and food in Pépin's kitchen. On a whim I sent the poem to Darra Goldstein at *Gastronomica*, who accepted it for their Winter 2004 issue. She also let me know that she'd shown the poem to Mr. Pépin—and that he enjoyed it. In the end, I outgrew my kitchen envy and learned to appreciate Claudine Pépin's taste in wine.

"I continue to nurse full-blown crushes on chefs Mario Batali, Eric Ripert, and Anthony Bourdain."

JAMES CUMMINS was born in Columbus, Ohio, in 1948, and grew up in the Midwest, primarily in Cleveland and Indianapolis. He received a BA from the University of Cincinnati and an MFA from the University of Iowa Writers' Workshop. His first book, *The Whole Truth*, was published by North Point Press in 1986; and his second, *Portrait in a Spoon*, by the University of South Carolina Press in 1997. *The Whole Truth* was reissued in the Carnegie-Mellon University Press's Classic Contemporary Series in 2003. His most recent book, *Then & Now*, was published by Swallow Press (Ohio University Press, 2004). A fourth book, *Jim and Dave Defeat the Masked Man*, written in collaboration with David Lehman and collecting most of the sestinas written by the two poets, with illustrations by the painter Archie Rand, will be published by Soft Skull Press in 2005. Cummins has been curator of the Elliston Poetry Collection at the University of Cincinnati since 1975, where he is also professor of English. He lives in Cincinnati with his wife, Maureen Bloomfield, and their daughters, Katherine and Margaret.

Of "The Poets March on Washington," Cummins writes: "This little satire came from three things: rereading with another poet, through much laughter, James Tate's poem, 'Lewis and Clark Overheard in Conversation,' which consists of one line, 'then we'll get us some wine and spare ribs,' repeated twenty-three times; remembering the huge protest march on Washington, D.C., after the Cambodia offensive in 1970; and musing, usually in the morning shower, on various senses of entitlement."

JAMEY DUNHAM was born in Kettering, Ohio, in 1973. He graduated from Miami University in 1996 and received his MFA from Bennington College in 1999. He teaches English at Sinclair Community College in Dayton, Ohio, and lives in Cincinnati with his wife and their son and daughter. His "An American Story" was included in the anthology *Great American Prose Poems: From Poe to the Present* (Scribner, 2003).

Of "Urban Myth," Dunham writes: "I had always been aware of the loose connection between the fable and the prose poem, so one day I decided to take a lemur down that road to see where it would lead. I love lemurs, all animals really, they make more sense to me than most people do. For me, the funny thing about this poem is the reaction it gets when I read it. People laugh and nod their heads agreeably, then push their strollers out of the bookstore in search of a suede blazer for their one-year-old. The poem scares me because I see it every day. I do, however, think of the lemur from time to time. I hope it's doing well for itself."

STEPHEN DUNN was born in Forest Hills, New York, in 1939. He is the author of thirteen books of poetry, including *The Insistence of Beauty* (2004) and *Different Hours*, both from W. W. Norton. The latter won the 2001 Pulitzer Prize. He is a professor of creative writing at Richard Stockton College of New Jersey, but spends most of his time in western Maryland, where he lives with his wife, the writer Barbara Hurd.

Of "Five Roses in the Morning," Dunn writes: "I wrote the poem on March 16, 2003, and dated it so because it was the eve of the Iraq war, a fact that seems more obscene to me now than then. My wife and I were honeymooning in St. Croix, a happy occasion mitigated by what we saw on television. So it's a kind of melancholy love poem, a lament about the war linked with the memory of a lovely evening, one event intruding into the other. The roses—reduced to five—remind me of the missing rose, which my wife wore in her hair the night before. Something poignant about that, a little thing that changed the evening for us, while elsewhere people were helpless to change what was on course to ruin their lives. Nothing profound, just a little moment enacted, a tone piece."

KARL ELDER was born in Beloit, Wisconsin, in 1948. He is a professor of creative writing and poet-in-residence at Lakeland College. His seven collections of poetry include *A Man in Pieces* (Prickly Pear Press, 1994), *The Geocryptogrammatist's Pocket Compendium of the United States* (Robert Schuricht Endowment Editions, 2001), *The Minimalist's How-to-Handbook* (Parallel Press, 2005), and *Mead: Twenty-six Abecedariums* (Marsh River Editions, 2005). From its inception, he has been associated with the literary magazine *Seems*—originally as a contributor, followed by poetry editor and, since 1978, editor and publisher. A member of the National Eagle Scout Association and a Vigil Honor member of the Order of the Arrow, Elder is active in scouting. He lives with his wife, Brenda, in Howards Grove, Wisconsin.

Of "Everything I Needed to Know," Elder writes: "I tell students that a poem is a poem, in part, by virtue of being unlike all other poems. But this dictum has a dark side. It served me for a couple of decades as a self-righteous explanation for why my work assumed such varied shapes and why I wasn't at all what one could call prolific. I could not find my pen through my pipe smoke.

"'Tedium is the worst pain,' says John Gardner's Grendel. Tired of waiting passively for the muse to flutter by my ear on her way to sit on the shoulders of others, I began blindly to invent, as I aimed for a pre-determined number of syllables per line. When one day in one of my notebooks (brand name Mead) it struck me to count the blank, ruled lines, it was as if the Ouija board in James Merrill's *Divine Comedies*, a volume I had laboriously and lovingly absorbed two dozen years before, suddenly spoke: 'U shall write in acrostics. U shall write a sequence of 26 poems of 26 lines in acrostics. U shall adhere with each piece to 260 syllables, ten per line. For a long, long while, U shall not be bored.'

"'But what shall I write *about*?' I asked.

"'Anything or everything,' the voice said. 'Choose.'

"Instant license.

"I chose, early on, to call the sequence *Mead*. After all, I compose initial drafts in a spiral notebook with a ready-made title printed on the cover. I check books out of Mead Library over in Sheboygan. I like honey wine—its hue, in particular. Mead is a pivotal prop in one of my favorite novels (Golding's *The Inheritors*). My wife and I fly over Lake Mead on our way to Vegas. And just the other day, I happened to look up at a street sign to find myself on Mead Avenue.

"When a friend asked me whether I think of myself as a formalist, I replied, 'I just want to evolve.'"

LYNN EMANUEL was born in Mt. Kisco, New York, in 1949. She holds a BA from Bennington College and an MFA from the University of Iowa. She is the author of three books of poetry: *Hotel Fiesta* (University of Georgia Press, 1984), *The Dig* (University of Illinois Press, 1992), and *Then, Suddenly* (University of Pittsburgh Press, 1999). She has taught at the Bread Loaf Writers' Conference, the Bennington Writing Seminars, the Warren Wilson Program in Creative Writing, and the Vermont College Writing Program. She is a professor of English at the University of Pittsburgh.

ELAINE EQUI was born in Oak Park, Illinois, in 1953. She is the author of *Surface Tension, Decoy, Voice-Over*, and most recently, *The Cloud of Knowable Things*, all from Coffee House Press. She teaches in the New School's MFA Writing program and in the graduate program at City College in New York City, where she lives with her husband, the poet Jerome Sala.

Of "Pre-Raphaelite Pinups," Equi writes: "I remember reading somewhere that Bob Perelman wrote his poem 'China' by looking at a book of photographs and writing captions. It sounded like a great idea and I knew immediately I wanted to do it. I've always been interested in the way words and pictures interact. For me the connection goes back in an almost primal way to how we're taught to read. One day while going through some old books, I rediscovered a collection of Pre-Raphaelite paintings called *The English Dreamers*. It was a book from the 1970s that had been a favorite of mine, probably because the reproductions not only evoked nineteenth-century decadence but also seemed to capture the look of glamorous hippies in late psychedelic splendor. It so happens that many of the paintings in this book were illustrations of poems. So in a sense, what my exercise does is return them to their original form."

CLAYTON ESHLEMAN was born in Indianapolis, Indiana, in 1935. From 1981 to 2000, he served as editor of *Sulfur*, putting out forty-six issues in all of this journal committed to experimental writing. For the past thirty years he has been doing research on what he calls "Upper Pale-olithic Imagination & the Construction of the Underworld." In 2003, Wesleyan University Press published the fruits of his research, *Juniper Fuse*. He has also published thirteen collections of poetry with Black Sparrow Press, the most recent being *My Devotion* (2004). In the spring of 2005, Soft Skull published his selected translations, *Conductors of the Pit*. In 2006, the University of California Press will publish his translation of *The Complete Poetry of César Vallejo*, with an introduction by Mario Vargas Llosa.

Of "The Magical Sadness of Omar Cáceres," Eshelman writes: "See Eliot Weinberger's essay, 'Omar Cáceres,' in *Karmic Traces* (New Directions, 2000). According to Weinberger, Cáceres is one of many significant and forgotten twentieth-century Latin American poets. He is known only by a collection of fifteen poems published by his brother in Chile in 1934. In his essay, Weinberger translates one of these poems, and this translation, along with the little information there is on the poet's life, moved me to write my own poem in the voice of Omar Cáceres."

ANDREW FELD was born in Cambridge, Massachusetts, in 1961. He holds a BA from the University of Massachusetts at Boson, and an MFA from the University of Houston. He has also received a Stegner Fellowship from Stanford University. *Citizen*, his first poetry collection, was chosen by Ellen Bryant Voigt for the National Poetry Series and was published by HarperCollins in 2004. Feld teaches at Carthage College and lives in Racine, Wisconsin, with his wife, the poet Pimone Triplett, and their son, Lukas.

Feld writes: "'19—: an Elegy' was written as the third part of a poem (entitled 'Best & Only') concerned with the distortions of language under political pressures, the difficulties of viewing past events through this distorting medium, and the pleasures of looking back through such a crazed lens. At some point during the writing of the first section, a narrative poem about the great love between Richard Nixon and his 'Best & Only' friend 'Bebe' Rebozo, I realized that the poem was going to end with an elegy for the twentieth century in the form of an abecedarium. As with any associative form, the poem rode out on the energy of its writing. I went to sleep one night, planning to write the poem in the morning, and as soon as the light was off, three or four pieces of the list came to me. I got up, wrote them down, and went back to bed. Then a few more came to me. In this way, yo-yoing back and forth between bed and living-room table, I finished the poem in less than an hour, with the exception of the lightbulb joke, which I added in the morning."

BETH ANN FENNELLY was born in Cranford, New Jersey, in 1971, and grew up in a suburb north of Chicago. She is currently an assistant professor of English at Ole Miss and lives in Oxford, Mississippi, with her husband, the fiction writer Tom Franklin, and their daughter, Claire. Her book *Open House* (Zoo Press, 2002) won the *Kenyon Review* Prize in Poetry. Her second book, *Tender Hooks*, was published by W. W. Norton in April, 2004.

Of "I Need to Be More French. Or Japanese," Fennelly writes: "When my first book was about to be published, my editor called me with the good news that a very chic Parisian designer had agreed, as a favor to him, to do the cover. I couldn't wait to see what she came up with. In just a few days, her mock-up arrived via e-mail attachment. And it was heartbreakingly ugly.

"Now I was in a dilemma because I wanted to like everything, to be an accommodating author. So I decided to learn to like the cover. I printed out a color copy and wrapped it around a book jacket, hoping to find it attractive. I failed. I slipped it in my bookshelf, pretending to come upon it after perusing a few other covers. Still butt ugly.

"About this time my editor called, wanting to know why he hadn't heard from me. I explained that I, um, wasn't sure that I fully appreciated the designer's vision. So he offered to have her phone me. Great.

Then the phone rang: *I hear you don't like my cover*, she said from stylish Paris. *What area code is 662 anyway?* When I said *Mississippi*, I heard the condescension in her voice as she replied that her designs *aren't for everyone, they're subtle.*

"I was chagrined, I was ashamed. I had bad taste! I never knew. I thought of all my garish habits and berated myself liberally. This lasted for a day or two. But gradually, I began to get a little feisty, thinking about the tyranny of people who live in fashionable places. So one morning I wrote this bitchy little poem and felt better immediately. Then I designed my own damn cover."

EDWARD FIELD was born in Brooklyn, New York, in 1924. He began writing poetry during World War II, when, as a navigator in the Eighth Air Force, he was stationed in England and flew twenty-five bombing missions over Germany. In 1962, his first book of poems, *Stand Up, Friend, with Me*, received the Lamont Award from the Academy of American Poets. The documentary *To Be Alive*, for which he wrote the narration, was shown at the New York World's Fair in 1964 and '65 and won an Academy Award. In 1992, he received a Lambda Award for *Counting Myself Lucky: Selected Poems 1963–1992* (Black Sparrow, 1992). Field and his partner, the novelist Neil Derrick, longtime residents of Greenwich Village, have written a best-selling historical novel, *The Villagers*, which tells the story of four generations of a Greenwich Village family along with the history of the Village and its development as the center of bohemia. His literary memoir, *The Man Who Would Marry Susan Sontag, and Other Intimate Literary Portraits of the Bohemian Era*, was published by the University of Wisconsin Press in 2004.

Of "In Praise of My Prostate," Field writes: "Though a friend of mine, a famous editor, warned me about writing one grim poem about old age after another, I have to admit that old age is one of my main subjects now that I'm well into the Oldie category. It's irresistible to write about, given that it's so unexpected, as Leon Trotsky once said. Coping with the manifestations and difficulties of old age starts absorbing one completely— it's a full-time job! Most people spend a lot of time consulting doctors, but I like to explore, and deal with, my 'condition' myself. It's me, after all, so why should I ask anyone else what I'm about? The body is changing in every way, and in this poem I'm thinking about sexuality and how it is in some ways better now—or at least is one of the abiding consolations."

RICHARD GARCIA was born in San Francisco, California, in 1941. He teaches for the Antioch low-residency graduate writing program in Los Angeles. He is also on the staff of the Idyllwild Poetry Festival in California. His books include *The Flying Garcias* (University of Pittsburgh Press, 1993), *Rancho Notorious* (BOA Editions, 2001), and the forthcoming volume, *The Persistence of Objects* (BOA Editions, 2006). He lives in Charleston, South Carolina.

Of "Adam and Eve's Dog," Garcia writes: "This poem was partly inspired by my dog Louie, who has a white tip on his tail. Dogs, because of their association with humans, are somewhat separated from their animal nature. They are thus on a journey of consciousness just as we are. 'Adam and Eve's Dog' began as an ekphrastic poem, based on works of art that I remembered seeing. After I wrote the poem, I attempted to look up the art—by Gustave Doré, for example—but found that the pieces in my mind did not exist. So the poem is an ekphrastic poem based on a false memory of popular iconography."

AMY GERSTLER was born in San Diego, California, in 1956. She currently teaches at the Bennington Writing Seminars at Bennington College and at Art Center College of Design in Los Angeles. Her books of poetry include *Ghost Girl* (Penguin, 2004), *Medicine* (Penguin, 2000), *Crown of Weeds* (Penguin, 1997), *Nerve Storm* (Penguin, 1993), and *Bitter Angel* (North Point Press, 1990; reissued by Carnegie-Mellon University Press). In addition to poetry, she writes art criticism and nonfiction, and does a variety of kinds of journalism.

Gerstler writes: "'Watch' is a poem consisting mostly of reportage. My father died of a heart attack in 2002. I wanted very much after that to write about him, to produce some kind of elegy for him, and was never able to do so. I thought that perhaps the best way for me to deal with his death and my grief about it would be through writing, but every time I tried I got helpless, stricken, and speechless. This little poem is as close as I have gotten so far, and there is very little of him or his spirit in it. Instead it deals with a small incident in the aftermath of his death, and trains its attention on an inanimate object, as a sort of stand-in for the man. His watch was the only item he was wearing at the time of his death that the coroner's office returned to us. (Apparently they dispose of the deceased's clothes in most cases.) For some strange reason I had wanted to have his shoes, the shoes he was wearing when he died—I have no idea why; maybe I just wanted to keep something that was touching him—and was sad to learn they had been incinerated or met whatever fate the discarded clothes of the dead meet in coroners' offices. After my mother and I drove to pick up my father's watch, she decided at the last minute not to go into the office, so I fetched it while she waited in the car. When I returned she was asleep. A few days later she told me she didn't want to keep that watch (he had several others) and gave it to me. It's hanging from a small nail on the wall of my office. A modest, inexpensive watch with a worn brown band. I can see it as I type this."

LEONARD GONTAREK was born in Philadelphia, Pennsylvania, in 1949, lived for some time in Vermont, and now lives in Philadelphia. He edited the City Books Broadside Series, 1992–95, and directed the Philadelphia Poetry Festival, 2002–3. His publications include *St. Genevieve Watching over Paris* (Telephone Books Press, 1984), *Van Morrison Can't Find His Feet* (My Pretty Jane Press, 1996), and *Zen for Beginners* (Green Bean Press, 2000). A new book, tentatively titled *I Don't Care What I Eat as Long as It's Every Day*, will be published by Autumn House Press in 2006.

Gontarek writes: "'Blue on Her Hands' came at the end of a long period of writing shorter poems. It surely had the feeling of arrival and departure. It is, along with the group of poems completed at the time, approximately a triptych. In poetry I like the power of making rules I can break. The poem attempts to make all connections, though it recognizes this as an impossibility. The same belief system, I confess, I use to negotiate the world. I am in the habit of telling my son my dreams, actual and invented. Revising your dreams isn't tampering. Rather it's a way of gaining access to truth. Choosing to tell the therapist another's dream in the poem is, it seem to me, not unlike other choices we make in our seductive, chaotic lives. Regarding the unfortunate fireworks boy in the poem: an early encounter with legend, it remains with me."

JESSICA GOODHEART was born in Boston, Massachusetts, in 1967. She graduated from Columbia College in 1989, and received a master's degree in urban planning from the University of California, Los Angeles, in 1995. She is a research director at the Los Angeles Alliance for a New Economy, a nonprofit organization dedicated to improving the lives of low-wage workers. She lives in northeast Los Angeles.

Goodheart writes: "'Advice for a Stegosaurus' emerged from a resonant phrase, not from any preconceived idea of the poem's final meaning. I could not have set out to write a poem about our threatened species and produced anything readable. Rather, I had a simple childish phrase stuck in my head, one that was ultimately dropped from the poem. During a summer trip to Mexico, our host used to entertain my three-year-old son at mealtime by saying, 'Don't eat me, dinosaur.' My first draft included that phrase and resembled a nursery rhyme. As I worked on the poem, the darker implications of what I was writing became apparent."

GEORGE GREEN was born in Grove City, Pennsylvania, in 1950. He received an MFA in poetry from the New School and currently teaches poetry and literature at Lehman College (CUNY) in the Bronx. His poems have appeared in the Random House anthologies *Poetry 180* and *180 More*.

Green writes: "When you write a poem about a work of art it's easy to find the devil in the details. To what extent should one describe the Grecian urn or the archaic torso? *The Searchers* is a fairly well-known film, but I decided to go with a synopsis. In the golden age of the revival house, New Yorkers could catch *The Searchers* in a good print on the big screen. Those days are gone, and I'm afraid the movie's 'cosmic grandeur' is not so 'sweeping' in DVD.

"During production John Wayne was often the worse for wear after late-night drinking bouts with director John Ford. The hangovers helped Wayne look anguished and haggard in what turned out to be his best performance.

"Jeffrey Hunter starred in the original pilot of *Star Trek*. Had he gone on to play Captain Kirk in the series, he would have become a pop-culture icon. Hunter supposedly declined the role, but, according to Leonard Nimoy, the producers were fed up with the demands of his 'pushy' second wife, Dusty Bartlett. Hunter's career just went downhill after *King of Kings*."

ARIELLE GREENBERG was born in Columbus, Ohio, in 1972, and has spent much of her life in upstate New York and New York City. She is now back in the Midwest: in Evanston, Illinois. She is the author of *Given* (Verse, 2002), and the chapbook *Fa(r)ther Down: Songs from the Allergy Trials* (New Michigan, 2003); she has also edited a college composition reader on subcultures and is coeditor, with Rachel Zucker, of a forthcoming anthology of essays by young women poets on their mentors and influences (Wesleyan University Press). This is her second appearance in *The Best American Poetry* series. She is a professor in the poetry program at Columbia College Chicago, a coeditor of the magazine *Court Green*, and poetry editor for *Black Clock*. She lives with her husband, Rob Morris.

Of "The Turn of the Screw," Greenberg writes: "I wrote this poem in the summer of 2002 while I was a fellow at the wonderful and generous MacDowell Colony. I was surrounded by brilliant artists, which was exhilarating and also intimidating, like a middle school dance. So I was thinking about aesthetics, and how Henry James's *The Turn of the Screw* is an enormous influence on my own: I first read it in my twelfth-grade honors English class, and our teacher spent the unit trying to get a bunch of repressed, hyperarticulate, socially inept kids to say out loud that the book was about lust. I was taken with the Freudian analysis we read, which said that Miss Jessel's ghost appears by a lake because lakes are womanly, vaginal lack, and Quint appears by a tower because it's phallic. Anyway, while at MacDowell, I formed a 'perverted movie club' with Amie Siegel, a poet and filmmaker, and Steve Erickson, a fiction writer and film critic: we discussed movies over breakfast. One of the films we talked about was Robert Altman's *Short Cuts*, and I remember saying that Julianne Moore's vagina—in a brief nude scene—was the best actor in the film. This isn't really true, of course, but it's like a ghost story, or a brief nude scene: it gives a little shock. In any case, this poem is an ars poetica."

MARILYN HACKER was born in New York City in 1942. She is the author of twelve books of poems, most recently, *Desesperanto*, which Norton published in 2003 with *First Cities: Collected Early Poems*. She received the Lenore Marshall Award of the Academy of American Poets in 1995 for *Winter Numbers*. She has translated the poetry of Claire Malroux and Vénus Khoury-Ghata. She lives in New York and Paris, and teaches at the City College of New York and the CUNY Graduate Center.

Of "For Kateb Yacine," Hacker writes: "The Algerian dramatist, poet, and novelist Kateb Yacine, a lifelong humanist militant, who died at sixty of leukemia in 1989, was one of the most innovative writers of the twentieth century in both French and Arabic. His trajectory went from literary success in fiction and experimental theater in France to ambitious large-scale productions in popular Arabic intended to give his own people back a sense of their history. His refusal of all orthodoxies, his wit, linguistic daring, and engagement make him a compelling figure. He regarded his many years in France as an exile: in this poem he joins a trans-temporal community of threatened exiles whose work resonates in the shadow of war, repression, and nationalism."

MATTHEA HARVEY was born in Bad Homburg, Germany, in 1973. She lived in England until the age of eight and then moved to Milwaukee. Her two books of poetry are *Pity the Bathtub Its Forced Embrace of the Human Form* (Alice James Books, 2000) and *Sad Little Breathing Machine* (Graywolf Press, 2004). She is the poetry editor of *American Letters & Commentary* and teaches at Sarah Lawrence College and the Warren Wilson MFA program. She lives in Brooklyn with her husband, Rob Casper, and their cat, Wednesday.

Harvey writes: "The title of this poem, 'I May After Leaving You Walk Quickly or Even Run,' is something my husband said to me as he ran off to I-don't-remember-where. There was something about the music of the phrase that I immediately loved—the way the iambs seemed to succumb to trochees, but then triumphed in the end. Ta da! I also liked how ambiguous the sentence was: the 'I' might be running out of joy or fear. The poem is an unhelpful daisy, whose every petal means both 'he loves me' and 'he loves me not.'"

STACEY HARWOOD was born in 1955 in New York City and educated at the University at Albany. She has a graduate degree in regulatory economics from the University at Albany and an MFA in writing and literature from Bennington College. For twenty-five years, Harwood has worked as a consumer advocate and policy analyst with the New York State Public Service Commission, the agency that regulates gas, electric, telephone, and water utilities in New York. She lives in New York City.

Of "Contributors' Notes," Harwood writes: "I'm interested in mini-forms of biography and autobiography—magazine interviews, obituaries, wedding announcements, contributors' notes—because of how carefully the information revealed by and about the individual is edited. I like to imagine the withheld side of each character in this poem: the baker as a narcissistic publicity hound, the dog trainer as controlling recluse, and so on. These characters also share the impulse to write about what they do, hence the reason for the Note to begin with. I experimented with different names, but found it easier to let my imagination go when using my own name for each note, probably because I've spent a lot of time dreaming up different lives for myself."

TERRANCE HAYES was born in Columbia, South Carolina, in 1971. He is the author of *Hip Logic* (Penguin, 2002) and *Muscular Music* (Tia Chucha Press, 1999). He teaches at Carnegie-Mellon University in

Pittsburgh, Pennsylvania, where he lives with his wife, the poet Yona Harvey, and their children, Ua and Aaron.

Of "Variations on Two Black Cinema Treasures," Hayes writes: "When I consider this poem retrospectively, I think of the word *ekphrasis*, which is generally defined as poetry about art or poetry concerned with the aesthetics of looking. But I suppose the word could apply to a hell of a lot of poetry, so maybe it's not that special. In any event, I found G. William Jones's *Black Cinema Treasures: Lost and Found* (University of North Texas Press, 1991) in a used bookstore one day. The book is full of details about black filmmakers and filmmaking of the 1920s through the 1950s. Especially interesting are the synopses of short films during that period. Somehow I got to imagining I was in a couple of them. So far only *Broken Earth* and *Boogie Woogie Blues* have climbed out of my ruminations. Are the two parts in dialogue? Does their juxtaposition create a clean singular meaning for the poem? No . . . I mean, yes, but who am I to tell you how to read?"

SAMUEL HAZO was born in Pittsburgh, Pennsylvania, in 1928. He is the founder and director of the International Poetry Forum in Pittsburgh, and is also McAnulty Distinguished Professor of English Emeritus at Duquesne University, where he has taught for forty-three years. His most recent books of poetry are *A Flight to Elsewhere* (2004) and *Just Once: New and Previous Poems* (2003), both from Autumn House Press. Other titles include a novel, *Stills* (Atheneum, 1989, rpt. Syracuse University Press); two dramas, *Feather* (1996) and *Mano a Mano* (2001); and a collection of essays, *Spying for God* (Byblos Press, 1999). He has translated Denis de Rougemont's *The Growl of Deeper Waters*, Nadia Tuéni's *Lebanon: Twenty Poems for One Love*, and Adonis' *The Pages of Day and Night*. He was chosen the first State Poet of the Commonwealth of Pennsylvania by Governor Robert Casey in 1993, and served until 2003.

Hazo writes: "'Seesaws' almost created itself as a litany of balances, but all the balances seemed in conflict. Each of the things listed created its opposite, but there was always more there than simple opposition. The more I wrote, the more the irony became apparent to me. It was an irony that reminded me of a comment of Aristotle in the *Poetics* that the essence of drama (read: life) was the presence therein of a seeming contradiction; that the worst, for example, always happens when we think the worst is over; and that there is always a discrepancy between appearance and reality. This applies to what I'm writing now—the longer the explanation, the less it is needed."

ANTHONY HECHT was born in New York City in 1923. After graduating from Bard College in 1944, he served in the infantry in World War II and witnessed the liberation of concentration camps. Hecht once described his work as "Formalist. Ironic. Oh yes: there's a certain amount of darkness to a lot of my poetry. It deals sometimes with very terrible aspects of experience." He praised Richard Wilbur for his mastery of "stately measure, cadences of a slow, processional grandeur, and rich, ceremonial orchestration," and this was true of Hecht as well. His books of poetry include *The Darkness and the Light* (Knopf, 2001); *Flight Among the Tombs* (1996); *The Transparent Man* (1990); *Collected Earlier Poems* (1990); *The Venetian Vespers* (1979); *Millions of Strange Shadows* (1977); *The Hard Hours* (1967), which won the Pulitzer Prize; and *A Summoning of Stones* (1954). He also wrote *On the Laws of Poetic Art: The Andrew Mellon Lectures, 1992* (1995) and *Obbligati: Essays in Criticism* (1986). He translated Aeschylus' *Seven Against Thebes* in collaboration with Helen Bacon (1975). He invented the double dactyl as a light verse form and he edited *Jiggery-Pokery: A Compendium of Double Dactyls* with John Hollander (1967). Hecht died of lymphoma in 2004.

JENNIFER MICHAEL HECHT was born in New York in 1965. *Funny*, her most recent poetry book, won the University of Wisconsin Press's Felix Pollak Poetry Prize for 2005. Her first collection of poems, *The Next Ancient World*, was published by Tupelo Press in 2001, and won the Poetry Society of America's Norma Farber First Book Award. She has also written two books of philosophy and history: *Doubt: A History* (Harper SanFrancisco, 2003) is a study of religious and philosophical doubt, all over the world, throughout time. *The End of the Soul: Scientific Modernity, Atheism, and Anthropology in France* (Columbia University Press, 2003) won the Phi Beta Kappa Society's Ralph Waldo Emerson Award "for scholarly studies that contribute significantly to interpretations of the intellectual and cultural condition of humanity." She is now writing "Modern Happiness: Insights from the History of Science, Society, and Culture" (or, perhaps, "Modern Happiness: An Exposé") for publication in late 2006. She lives in Brooklyn with her husband and young son.

Of "The Propagation of the Species," Hecht writes: "I wrote this poem when I was deciding whether the next thing I wanted to do in my life was motherhood. When I read it now, I'm a little surprised at how much the issue of worry was on my mind. Look how I keep talking about odds, statistics, and danger. Now, I'll tell you, I have Max, seven months old at this writing, and most of the time he seems pretty sturdy to me. The world may be tough, but I think he's the man for the job.

"This poem belongs to my new book, *Funny*, and like most of the poems in *Funny* it has an old joke embedded in it—this time the one about the sloth and the hooligan snails. I have always been distracted by time. On the train platform I imagine the train coming, then I imagine being nestled in my seat with my newspaper and beverage, then the walk, then home at last. But I don't stop there, I fast-forward to the next time I'm waiting on a platform. Then, still waiting for the train, I realize that I am now in the satisfied, has-already-got-home-and-left again future of some past wait on the platform. It is difficult to stay put in time under these circumstances. It's as Keats said, 'If a sparrow come before my window, I take part in its existence, and pick about the gravel.'

"Then this joke came along and as I gave it thought I discovered that it was all about time and how it feels when it's passing through you, the way you're young and in school forever, and then one day you're not—forever. Also, the strangeness of the world after a big change has occurred in the individual life. I'm not sure if it's because adult humans are hypnotized most of the time, then when they travel or when the big wave comes, they are shocked back to an infantlike marveling, weeping, and laughing.

"The jokes in the poems made me laugh when I heard them, and got deep and resonant when I spent time with them. Things that were on my mind would show themselves to have something in common with the joke, and the poems got woven. They're all personal as well as philosophical, but this one is among the most autobiographical. The sloth getting attacked by snails and experiencing it as happening too fast to register reminded me, after a while, of how these big decisions seem to work: endless hesitation, and then suddenly, in a flash, the choice is long behind you and you are decidedly elsewhere, stunned at what all the mulling was over.

"Now here I am on the other side of the experience I was considering, having made the decision and seen my desire enacted, and I am exceedingly pleased. Furthermore, I can now report that I have been right about nearly everything. What are the exceptions? Well, we all know we're wasting about half our time on the planet, we're just not sure which half. In any case, my advice remains the same: study verse, risk failure, pack a lunch. If you become a sparrow, you still may not want to eat bugs, and even a poet needs to eat."

LYN HEJINIAN was born at the Alameda Naval Base, in Northern California, in 1941. Her most recent books are *My Life in the Nineties* (Shark, 2003) and *The Fatalist* (Omnidawn, 2003). She is the editor of Tuumba Press and the coeditor of Atelos. She teaches in the English department at the University of California, Berkeley. She was the guest editor of *The Best American Poetry 2004*.

Hejinian writes: "The four-part sequence printed here is part of a book-length work, *The Fatalist*, which is derived entirely from all the letters and e-messages (as well as a few blurbs and introductions to poetry readings) that I wrote over the course of one year. For the duration of that year, I pasted the texts of all my communications with others into a single file, keeping the chronology intact. I then went back to the beginning of the file, and by massively deleting and obsessively lineating (and without adding anything or moving anything around), I sculpted the poems out of the raw epistolary material. My only other editorial intervention involved substituting letters for names, so as to protect the privacy of people I wrote to or wrote about. Not all of the letters correspond to the letters in the name of the original.

"If one defines 'fate' retrospectively (as all that has happened and thus all that will never *not* have happened), then a record of what has happened (of the sort that might be set down over the course of a year in letters) is, arguably, an account of fate, and the giver of that account (and participant in it) a fatalist. Hence the title. Recording the unfolding of this version of fate was my primary interest in composing the work; a second interest was in intimacy and exteriority of address—in giving the account to an *other*, since the place of others (whether dear or contingent) in a life inevitably characterizes its fate."

RUTH HERSCHBERGER was born in Philipse Manor, New York, in 1917, and grew up in Chicago. She attended the University of Chicago and Black Mountain College. Her books of poems are *A Way of Happening* (Pellgrini & Cudahy, 1948) and *Nature & Love Poems* (Eakins Press, 1969). She is also the author of *Adam's Rib* (Pellgrini & Cudahy, 1948; pbk., Harper & Row, 1970), an important nonfiction book that anticipates the concerns of feminists a generation later.

JANE HIRSHFIELD was born in New York City in 1953. Her most recent poetry collection is *Given Sugar, Given Salt* (HarperCollins, 2001). A new volume, her sixth, will come out from HarperCollins in early 2006. She has also written a collection of essays, *Nine Gates: Entering the Mind of*

Poetry (HarperCollins, 1997), and has edited three volumes collecting the work of women poets from the past. She has taught in the Bennington College MFA Writing Program and at the University of California, Berkeley. She has lived in the San Francisco Bay Area since 1974.

TONY HOAGLAND was born in Tucson, Arizona, in 1953, and has moved so many times since, he can't remember where he's from. He currently teaches at the University of Houston and in the Warren Wilson College MFA program. *What Narcissism Means to Me* appeared from Graywolf Press in 2003. A selected poems by the same title was just published in the United Kingdom by Bloodaxe Books. A collection of prose about poetry, *Real Sofistakashun*, is en route.

Hoagland writes: "When 'In a Quiet Town by the Sea' was chosen for *BAP 2005*, I was, at first, dismayed, and considered declining the privilege of being published here. The poem was written a few years ago, and its subject matter, masculinity and sex, is sort of in my rearview mirror now. Craftwise, too, the poem seems a little hacked out to me. What, really, does it discover? Yet the poem does represent several of my ongoing poetic interests: the art of rudeness, the bafflements of gender, and the dialectical play of multiple tones and voices in a poem. Although 'In a Quiet Town by the Sea' did indeed arise from experience—listening one night to two of my married friends talk about temptation and infidelity—I value more the en route rhetorical transformations and ornaments of the poem. Maybe this poem is taking a look at the fossil record and, in some of its movements, maybe there is evidence of life."

VICKI HUDSPITH was born in picturesque Winterset, Iowa, in 1952. Her latest collection of poetry is in the form of a spoken-word CD, *URBAN VOODOO* (available from www.spdbooks.org). Her two previous collections, *White and Nervous* and *Limousine Dreams*, were published by Bench Press. In 1982 she directed two plays for Eye and Ear Theater, a collaborative theater of poets and visual artists in New York City. She directed *The Heroes* by John Ashbery, with sets by Jane Freilicher, and *Shopping and Waiting* by James Schuyler, with sets by Alex Katz. She was president of the artistic board of directors of the Poetry Project in New York City from 1985 to 2005 and currently serves on the board of the Bowery Poetry Club. She is writer-in-residence for both Teachers & Writers Collaborative and Urban Word in New York City, where she lives.

Of "Ants," Hudspith writes: "For the last several years, I have traded poems back and forth almost daily with the poet Frank Lima. He sent me a poem referencing crows, based on a Neruda poem. Ants were mentioned. I became fascinated by how archetypal these tiny insects were and embarked on writing about their 'secret lives.' It seemed that everyone was impressed with their hard work, but no one had ever attached an emotional value to that or their service to their queen.

"I decided to debunk various myths about ants. For example, ants and picnics. Do they enjoy them or do they feel that history requires them to put in an appearance at every picnic? I decided that if they were such workaholics, there might be other aspects of an ant's life that paralleled the human journey. From there on, the secret lives and lies about ants unfolded. They are much like us, it seems: they work too hard, don't understand why they do what they do, and like music they look ridiculous dancing to!

"It was the first piece I ever put to music. I worked out a drum track with the jazz musician and percussionist Daniel Freedman which emphasized ants in their relentless devotion to task and tribe. It's the first track on my CD *URBAN VOODOO*."

DONALD JUSTICE was born in Miami, Florida, in 1925. A graduate of the University of Miami, he later attended the universities of North Carolina, Stanford, and Iowa. His *Collected Poems* appeared from Knopf in 2004; *Selected Poems* (Knopf, 1979) received the Pulitzer Prize. Justice was not prolific. But what he wrote was consistently high in quality. He balanced the demands of traditional stanzas and forms (including the extravagant sestina and the rigorous villanelle) with the attractions of the American idiom. A deep romantic nostalgia, midway between sadness and tranquility, was his element. At the University of Iowa Writers' Workshop, where Justice taught for many years, his admiring students included Mark Strand, Charles Wright, and Jorie Graham. Strand did a pitch-perfect parody of the soulful Justice manner in a poem entitled "Nostalgia," which concludes, "It is yesterday. It is still yesterday." Many of Justice's poems live or lurk "in the shadows" (the concluding phrase of Justice's "On the Death of Friends in Childhood"). "The Tourist from Syracuse," originally published in 1967, acquired a scary new currency after the attacks of September 11. It is the portrait of a man who could be a used-car salesman, a tourist from Syracuse, or a hired assassin, who is waiting—"like one who has missed his bus"—at the "corner at which you turn / To approach that place where now / You must not hope to arrive."

Justice lived with his wife, Jean Ross, in Iowa City, until his death on August 6, 2004.

MARY KARR was born in southeast Texas in 1955. A Guggenheim Fellow, she teaches at Syracuse University. Her fourth book of poems, *Coathanger: Halo*, will be published by HarperCollins in 2006. Her best-selling memoirs are *The Liars' Club* (Viking, 1995) and *Cherry* (Viking, 2000).

GARRET KEIZER was born in Paterson, New Jersey, in 1953. A freelance writer, he is the author of four books of essays, *Help* (HarperCollins, 2004), *The Enigma of Anger* (Jossey-Bass, 2002), *A Dresser of Sycamore Trees* (Viking-Penguin, 1991), and *No Place But Here* (Viking-Penguin, 1988), as well as a short novel, *God of Beer* (HarperCollins, 2002). For many years he worked as a public school teacher and minister in northeastern Vermont.

Of "Hell and Love," Keizer writes: "I wrote this poem in a café while waiting for my lunch. Our thoughts range from hell to art, from love to heaven, but are seldom far from lunch. Lucky for us. The head on the plate is John the Baptist's and the Passion is Christ's. The painters are ours, along with all the questions they inspire."

BRIGIT PEGEEN KELLY was born in Palo Alto, California, in 1951. She teaches in the creative writing program at the University of Illinois, Urbana-Champaign. Her third book of poems, *The Orchard*, was published by BOA Editions in 2004.

GALWAY KINNELL was born in Providence, Rhode Island, in 1927. He is the author of nine books of poetry, including *The Book of Nightmares* (1973), *Imperfect Thirst* (1996), and *A New Selected Poems* (2001), all from Mariner books, and several translations, including *The Poems of François Villon* (University Press of New England, 1982) and *The Essential Rilke* (Ecco, 1999). He has been a MacArthur Fellow and State Poet of Vermont. In 1982 his *Selected Poems* won the Pulitzer Prize. He lives in New York City and in Vermont.

RACHEL LODEN was born in Washington, D.C., in 1948. She is the author of *Hotel Imperium* (University of Georgia Press, 1999). She has also published four chapbooks, including *The Richard Nixon Snow Globe* (Wild Honey Press, 2005). She lives in Palo Alto, California, and is completing her second full-length manuscript, "The Bride of Franken-stein."

Of "In the Graveyard of Fallen Monuments," Loden writes: "I had received a brochure from the National Geographic Society, offering a cruise of Russia and the Baltic. As something of a recluse, I'm partial to itineraries, so I noted with pleasure a stop at the Graveyard of Fallen Monuments. On the Web I discovered that the graveyard actually exists in Moscow and collects toppled statuary from the Soviet era, including a legless figure of Leonid Brezhnev (general secretary of the Communist Party of the Soviet Union from 1964 to 1982).

"I'd always felt a special connection with the countries of the former USSR since my paternal grandparents emigrated to the United States from Moscow and Kiev before the revolution. In the thirties, my grand-father returned to build socialism. Instead he found Stalin's terror-machine and mass starvation. He was lucky to escape with his life.

"It seemed likely that Richard Nixon would be excited and dis-turbed to find his old Soviet counterpart and yachting buddy in the Graveyard of Fallen Monuments. He would not be silenced by mere death. And so he had his say on this, as on everything else in our con-vulsively shifting world."

SARAH MANGUSO was born in Newton, Massachusetts, in 1974. Edu-cated at Harvard and the Iowa Writers' Workshop, she was the Hodder Fellow in poetry at Princeton in 2003–4. She is the author of *The Captain Lands in Paradise* (Alice James Books, 2002) and the forthcoming *Siste Via-tor* (Four Way Books, 2006). With Jordan Davis she coedited the anthol-ogy *Free Radicals: American Poets Before Their First Books* (Subpress, 2004). She teaches in the New School's MFA program, writes criticism for *The Believer*, and is at work on a third manuscript of poems entitled "The Guardians." She lives in Brooklyn, New York.

Of "Hell," Manguso writes: "The music I refer to in the fourth sec-tion (per my journal entry of 11/3/01, the day I wrote this poem) is the sound of Will Oldham singing 'I See a Darkness.'"

HEATHER MCHUGH was born in San Diego, California, in 1948. She teaches in the MFA program in creative writing at the University of Washington. Her latest book of poems is *Eyeshot* (Wesleyan University Press, 2003). A volume of her essays entitled *Broken English: Poetry and Partiality* appeared from Wesleyan in 1993.

Of "Ill-Made Almighty," McHugh writes: "I'm reasonably certain (though certainty's foolhardiness) that this poem is addressed to God, and not to myself. (I'm reasonably certain I can tell them apart. I think God isn't plagued by thinking. I hope God isn't plagued by hope.) If the heavens are adrift, I mean to address the yaw, the yawning maw."

D. NURKSE was born in New York City in 1949. He is the author of eight books of poetry, most recently *Voices over Water* (1996), *Leaving Xaia* (2000), and *The Rules of Paradise* (2001), all from Four Way Books, and *The Fall* (2002) and *Burnt Island* (2005), from Knopf. He teaches at Sarah Lawrence College and the Stonecoast MFA program.

Of "Space Marriage," Nurkse writes: "In the twenty-first-century vice-jaws of fundamentalism and consumerism—two boredoms—my mind has been drifting, with hungry ignorance, to other space/times. Some of these 'other dimensions' are perfectly real. I've been fascinated by Lyn Margulis and Karlene V. Schwartz's rigorously researched *Five Kingdoms: The Phyla of Life on Earth*, in which all mammals put together take up about one page out of four hundred, and there are probably a thousand kinds of 'natural' sex.

"In 'Space Marriage,' the premise is fictive. I used to watch TV over my nephew's shoulder. His programs seemed more interesting than my poems, and it wasn't the flickering lights on the screen, but the language, which I altered for my own purposes."

STEVE ORLEN was born in Holyoke, Massachusetts, in 1942. He is a professor of English at the University of Arizona and a visiting faculty member in the low-residency MFA program at Warren Wilson College. His books of poetry are *Permission to Speak* (Wesleyan University Press, 1978), *A Place at the Table* (Holt, Rinehart & Winston, 1981), *The Bridge of Sighs* (Miami University Press, 1992), *Kisses* (Miami University Press, 1997), and *This Particular Eternity* (Ausable Press, 2001). He "just finished a new manuscript of poems, and sent it out to some friends whose role is to keep me from making a fool of myself in print."

Of "I Love You. Who Are You?" Orlen writes: "The title came to me before the poem, as an obsessive koan repeated to myself over several months when I was fantasizing a lovelessness that wasn't actual. One night on television I saw Dolly Parton, who is among our best lyricists of country music. She was being interviewed on television, and I fell in love with her wit, intelligence, generosity, and quintessentially American ageless beauty. It so happened that the next morning I was reading some English ballads and fell in love with the music, and began to write this poem, a paean to Dolly. The fun was in the end-rhyming, which I'm not very good at, and the freedom was in refusing the call from the old ballad-makers to pattern it. It took about three years to get it where I wanted it."

EUGENE OSTASHEVSKY was born in 1968 in Leningrad. His family immigrated to New York in 1979. He is the author of *Iterature*, a book of poems appearing in 2005 from Ugly Duckling Presse, and of "The Book of DJ Spinoza," a poetry manuscript currently in search of a publisher. His translations of Russian absurdist poetry of the 1930s have appeared in *OBERIU: An Anthology of Russian Absurdism, 1927–1941* (Northwestern University Press, 2005), and Alexander Vvedensky's *Selected Works* (forthcoming from Green Integer). He has written a PhD dissertation on the concept of zero in the mathematics, philosophy, and literature of early modern Europe. He currently teaches in the general studies program of New York University. English is his second first language.

Ostashevsky writes: "'Dear Owl' is from my second poetry manuscript, 'The Book of DJ Spinoza.' Although DJ Spinoza does not appear in it, and neither do his nemeses the Begriffon and MC Squared, 'Dear Owl' is concerned with the same problem as the rest of the collection: how is it possible to make sense when it is not possible to make sense? I started working on the book after reading Spinoza's *Ethics*, which employs the geometrical method of proceeding from axioms to theorems in order to construct an exhaustive rationalist explanation of the world. *The Ethics* fails for several reasons: first of all, because the emergence of non-Euclidean geometry has relativized the concept of the axiom; second, because the collapse of the attempt to logicize the foundations of mathematics has shown the impossibility of constructing any exhaustive rationalist explanation: and, last—and this is the only fault Spinoza can really be charged with—because he assumes natural language can be employed as univocally as the artificial language of mathematics. (It is due to this howler that the *Ethics* may be read as philosophical slapstick.) What does any of this have to do with 'Dear Owl'? Well, 'Dear Owl' is about love—and love is a form of knowing that adamantly resists translation into any system of propositions, to the extent that, when you're in love, you can ask yourself, 'Am I in love, i.e., does that word apply to what I am feeling?' and it applies questioningly. But love occurs nonetheless. So the fact that something can't be translated into rational discourse without engendering paradoxes, doesn't imply that it's nonexistent or meaningless. Ascertaining this is especially important because every form of knowing becomes paradoxical if you rationalize it sufficiently. We can say that the fact that we love tells us there are moments when we do know the world, no matter how restricted our knowledge of it might be and no matter how much it offends our conception of knowledge, not having any ultimate axiomatic ground to stand on."

LINDA PASTAN was born in New York City in 1932, graduated from Radcliffe College in 1954, and received an MA from Brandeis University in 1957. She has published eleven volumes of poetry, most recently, *The Last Uncle* (W. W. Norton, 2002). Two of her books, *PM/AM* (1982) and *Carnival Evening* (1999), both from Norton, were finalists for the National Book Award. She was Poet Laureate of Maryland from 1991 to 1995 and received the Ruth Lilly Poetry Prize in 2003. For twenty years, she was on the staff of the Bread Loaf Writers' Conference.

Of "Death Is Intended," Pastan writes: "There is probably as little chance that I'll commit suicide one day as there is that I'll climb some mountain, particularly in winter. But reading about Guy Waterman, and the choice he made, gave me a feeling of liberating possibility—at least on the page."

ADRIENNE RICH was born in Baltimore in 1929. Her most recent books of poetry are *The School Among the Ruins: Poems 2000–2004* and *Fox: Poems 1998–2000*. A selection of her essays, *Arts of the Possible: Essays and Conversations*, was published in 2001. A new edition of *What Is Found There: Notebooks on Poetry and Politics* appeared in 2003. (These titles were all published by W. W. Norton.) She was the editor of *The Best American Poetry 1996* and of the *Selected Poems of Muriel Rukeyser* (Library of America). She has lived in New York City and New England, and for over twenty years in California.

Of "Dislocations: Seven Scenarios," Rich writes: "Although America was founded on dislocations—some voluntary, some desperate, mostly enforced—we persist in expecting familiarity and stability. My poem counterposes various displacements/disjunctures, of place and time, individual and collective, details from a larger fresco, or, perhaps, frames from a longer film.

"The sentence beginning *You thought you were innocent* is from Paul Nizan, *Aden Arabie* (New York: Monthly Review Press, 1979, p. 131)."

JAMES RICHARDSON was born in Bradenton, Florida, on January 1, 1950, and grew up in Garden City, New York. His recent books include

Interglacial: New and Selected Poems and Aphorisms (Ausable, 2004), *Vectors: Aphorisms and Ten-Second Essays* (Ausable, 2001), and *How Things Are* (Carnegie-Mellon University Press, 2000). He is a professor of creative writing and English at Princeton University.

Of "All the Ghosts," Richardson writes: "Some masochist once asked Thomas Hardy to reassure him about the Value of Life, and he got the reply he deserved: 'For my part, if there is any way of getting a melancholy satisfaction out of life it lies in dying, so to speak, before one is out of the flesh; by which I mean putting on the manners of ghosts, wandering in their haunts, and taking their views of surrounding things. To think of life as passing away is a sadness; to think of it as past is at least tolerable. Hence even when I enter into a room to pay a simple morning call I have unconsciously the habit of regarding the scene as if I were a spectre not solid enough to influence my environment; only fit to behold and say, as another spectre said: 'Peace be unto you!'

"As an inveterate admirer of such ghostly writers as Tennyson and the Rossettis, Swinburne and Hardy, I wouldn't be surprised if my ghosts were a little Victorian. They also seem to be precisonists, whether scientists or poets. And they might be any of us, watching the terrible news on television, or watching our lives as if on television, at once invulnerable and helpless."

MARY RUEFLE was born in McKeesport, Pennsylvania, in 1952. She is the author of eight books of poetry, most recently, *Tristimania* (Carnegie-Mellon University Press, 2004), and teaches in the MFA writing program at Vermont College. This is her third appearance in *The Best American Poetry*.

Of "How I Became Impossible," Ruefle writes: "I am a member of the cult of persons who devour books about our planet's antipodes, the North and South poles and their outlying icy zones; you say Amundsen, Freuchen, Shackelton, and I swoon. Yet I persisted in picturing the bears and birds together at both ends; after all, little plastic replicas of them frolicked together in my deep freeze. This poem is a true account of my shocking mistake, and its sobering aftermath. It seemed one more instance—despite the frivolity of cheerleaders who will tell you life is full of endless possibilities—that possibilities do diminish and keep diminishing, things become less and less possible as we age, until our lives are literally impossible, and we die. But as no poem is as cynical as its explanation, I will keep writing them."

KAY RYAN was born in California in 1945 and grew up in the small towns of San Joaquin Valley and the Mojave Desert. She studied at the Los Angeles and Irvine campuses of the University of California. Since 1971 she has lived in Marin County. She has published six books of poetry, including *Flamingo Watching* (Copper Beech Press, 1994), and *Elephant Rocks* (1996) and *Say Uncle* (2000), both from Grove Press. Her new book of poems, *The Niagara River*, will be published by Grove Press this year. Her work was included in the 1995 and 1999 volumes of *The Best American Poetry*, as well as in *The Best of the Best American Poetry 1988–1997*.

Ryan writes: "On September 11, 2001, 'Home to Roost' was in New York, sitting on the desk of a poetry editor.

"When I wrote the poem, months earlier, it was simply about how your choices can gang up, turn around, and go bad on you, a subject I was thinking about for personal reasons. But after 9/11, it seemed irresistible to read the poem as anything but a quite cold-blooded take on how American airplanes can be turned into weapons and set upon America, and how this nightmarish turn may be the result of America's own choices in the world. In the same group of poems I had submitted was another—now just as bad—which was about how when the worst possible thing has happened, salvagers come in and take apart the wreckage, stripping it of pain, reducing it to neutral elements, 'whistling as they work.' This second poem, too, was written months before 9/11.

"As soon as the phones to New York were up again, I called to withdraw the poems, now so cruel-sounding. They had been grotesquely distorted by the blast. I hated how an outside event could warp even the language of a poem, could rob me of my poem. I had wanted language to be unwarpable. And indeed language is strong and can reassert itself after a blow. Without this story, probably nobody reading 'Home to Roost' in this 2005 anthology would connect this poem to 9/11/01 as they surely, surely would have then."

JEROME SALA was born in 1951 in Evergreen Park, Illinois, and grew up in Chicago. Though slight of frame, he was crowned the first World Heavyweight Champion of Poetry in 1981. His books include cult classics such as *Spaz Attack* (STARE Press, 1980), *I Am Not a Juvenile Delinquent* (STARE Press, 1984), *The Trip* (Highlander Press, 1989), and *Raw Deal: New and Selected Poems* (Another Chicago Press, 1994). His new book, published last year by Soft Skull Press, is entitled

Look Slimmer Instantly! He lives in New York City with his wife, Elaine Equi.

Of "Media Effects," Sala writes: "For most of my adult life, I've written in two genres: advertising copy for money and poetry, for some reason not clear to myself. Naturally, I've wondered about the connection between them, as they seem very similar in some ways—both often depending on wit, brevity, and self-referential irony. Recently I came upon the writings of the late, great sociologist Pierre Bourdieu, who proved that while commercial writing supported a money economy, arty writing was locked in to an economy of its own—one that produced prestige instead of cash. I found this idea amusing enough to generate a poem."

MARY JO SALTER was born in Grand Rapids, Michigan, in 1954. She is Emily Dickinson Senior Lecturer in the Humanities at Mount Holyoke College and lives in Amherst, Massachusetts. She is coeditor, with Margaret Ferguson and Jon Stallworthy, of *The Norton Anthology of Poetry* (fourth and fifth editions). Her first play, *Falling Bodies*, was produced in 2004. She has written a children's book entitled *The Moon Comes Home* (Knopf, 1989), as well as five collections of poetry, also from Knopf, the most recent of which are *A Kiss in Space* (1999) and *Open Shutters* (2003).

Of "Costanza Bonarelli," Salter writes: "In listening to a recent lecture on Gian Lorenzo Bernini's celebrated bust of Costanza Bonarelli, I was mesmerized by one detail particularly: that the very artist who had created, with his chisel, an immortal marble image of his lover's face would later arrange to have another man slash her real face with a razor. Bernini went on, apparently, to destroy some of his loving images of the faithless Bonarelli. Yet his need to disfigure the original was what haunted me. I sought to make shapely stanzas, and to employ a language that was both highly sensual and refined, in imitation of Bernini; and I hoped my reader would be shocked, but on later reflection not so surprised, by the sudden transformation of sexual attraction into violence."

CHRISTINE SCANLON was born in New York City in 1971 and, except for a brief time in Montreal, has lived there ever since. She now lives in the Lower East Side of Manhattan. In 2003 she received her MFA from the New School and is currently pursuing further graduate studies at the City University of New York. She was awarded the 2003 Barrow Street Book Contest for her poetry collection *A Hat on the Bed*.

Of "The Grilled Cheese Sandwich," she writes: "Starting with the concept of the grilled cheese sandwich but unsure how to proceed, I turned to (where else?) Emily Post and her 1922 classic, *Emily Post: Etiquette in Society, in Business, in Politics and at Home*. Post was a great equalizer. Through the use of her language it becomes possible to elevate the grilled cheese sandwich above its comfort-food origins while making good manners accessible to everyone."

JASON SCHNEIDERMAN was born in San Antonio, Texas, in 1976. He holds bachelor's degrees in English and Russian from the University of Maryland, and received an MFA from New York University. His first collection of poems, *Sublimation Point*, was published by Four Way Books in 2004. He has twice been head waiter at the Bread Loaf Writers' Conference. He is a doctoral candidate in English at CUNY's Graduate Center and teaches creative writing at Hofstra University.

Of "Moscow," Schneiderman writes: "I should probably explain that I used to take myself on dates to Moscow. I was studying in St. Petersburg and had gotten involved with someone, but the relationship ended terribly (he was cheating with me on a championship skier). I used to take the night train to Moscow, where I could get real coffee and see all the foreign movies. I was extremely chivalrous, and really showed myself a good time. It was a nice time—I liked being in a foreign country and single. When I moved to New York, I fell in love, and I'm still in love. I like navigating a life for two, but sometimes it's harder to pick which movie to see."

JULIE SHEEHAN was born in Pierson, Iowa ("Pop. 500, Some Bigger, None Better"), in 1964. She holds several degrees: a bachelor of arts from Yale, a master of fine arts from Columbia, and an exercise in futility, which took ten years to complete, from New York City's downtown theater community. Her first book of poems, *Thaw*, was published by Fordham University Press in 2001. She lives a precarious freelance existence perched on the East End of Long Island like a migratory bird ignoring her instinct.

Of "Hate Poem," Sheehan writes: "It occurred to me, as probably to many, that since hate requires as much passion as love, the two emotions can be described in indistinguishable terms. The sagging lyrics of love songs snap right back into an elastic shape through a simple substitution of the word 'hate' for 'love,' as in the first line of this poem. (Thanks, Richard Howard!) Hate also demands of its bearer the same scrutinizing myopia: hence, the delight we take from inspecting each minute feature of the self in love and the beloved can be derived in equal measure from the self in hate and the be-hated (beheaded?). A list seemed the perfect form for this fit of passion, and the image for idealism at the end of the poem, that of lungs, another passionate pair, as dwelling in the broken submarine of the body, was one of those felicities visited upon you when you sit down to write, a felicity for which I can claim no credit, except that I *did* sit down to write instead of doing laundry or whatever other Futilities I undertake instead of writing hate poems."

CHARLES SIMIC was born in Belgrade, Yugoslavia, in 1938, and emigrated to the United States in 1954. A poet, essayist, and translator, he teaches American literature and creative writing at the University of New Hampshire. He has published seventeen collections of his own poems, five books of essays, a memoir, and numerous books of translations. He has received the MacArthur Fellowship and the Pulitzer Prize. His most recent books of poems, both from Harcourt, are *The Voice at 3 A.M.: Selected Late and New Poems* (2003) and *My Noiseless Entourage* (2005). He was guest editor of *The Best American Poetry 1992*.

Of "Sunlight," Simic writes: "There's nothing so obvious, so elusive and so difficult to describe as light. The way it comes in the morning and stops over a pair of old shoes and makes them beautiful to look at. There's truth in it and compassion, too. It tries to teach us to think, but we are slow learners. It's the first mystery and the last mystery. The poem is attempting to say something like that."

LOUIS SIMPSON was born in Jamaica, West Indies, in 1923, the son of a lawyer of Scottish descent and a Russian mother. He emigrated to the United States at the age of seventeen, studied at Columbia University, then served in the Second World War with the 101st Airborne Division on active duty in France, Holland, Belgium, and Germany. After the war he continued his studies at Columbia and the University of Paris. *The Owner of the House: New Collected Poems 1940–2001* (BOA Editions, 2003) was nominated for the Griffin Award and a National Book Award. He recently published two translations, *Modern Poets of France: A Bilingual Anthology* (1997) and François Villon's *The Legacy and the Testament* (2000), both from Story Line Press. Stewe Claeson has translated some of Simpson's poems into Swedish, *Kaviar påå begravningen* (Ordfront Föörlag, 1988). Simpson lives in Stony Brook, New York, with a beagle,

Lottie, whom he walks three times a day. Like Eliot, "he do the police in different voices." There aren't many diversions in Stony Brook.

W. D. SNODGRASS was born in Beaver Falls, Pennsylvania, in 1926, and spent much of his life teaching creative writing and oral interpretation, most recently at the University of Delaware. His more than twenty books of poetry include *The Fuehrer Bunker: The Complete Cycle* (BOA Editions, 1995); *Each in His Season* (BOA Editions, 1993); *Selected Poems, 1957–1987* (Soho Press, 1987); *The Führer Bunker: A Cycle of Poems in Progress* (BOA Editions, 1977), which was produced by Wynn Handman for The American Place Theatre. In 1959 he received a Pulitzer Prize for his first collection of poems, *Heart's Needle*. His most recent book of literary criticism is *De/Composition* (Graywolf Press, 2001) and his *Selected Translations* (BOA Editions, 1998) won the Harold Morton Landon Translation Award. He and his wife, Kathleen, divide their time between central New York and San Miguel de Allende, Mexico.

Of "For Hughes Cuenod—in his 100th year," Snodgrass writes: "The details of the poem are correct, if abbreviated; Nadia Boulanger was his teacher as well as director and manager. When Stravinsky heard Cuenod sing, he created a new part in *The Rake's Progress* for him. Friends of mine were present at the solo concert he improvised, filling in for an American singer who had a nervous breakdown.

"I never met Cuenod in person but many of my friends were students of his, especially from his master classes. Besides the charming card he wrote me on seeing this new poem, he once answered a letter I'd written, thanking him for the deep effect his singing had had on my poems. His answer took four years to reach me—following him all around the glove and getting stalled, occasionally, on agents' desks."

GARY SNYDER was born in San Francisco, California, in 1930. As a youth in the Pacific Northwest, he worked on the family farm and seasonally in the woods. He graduated from Reed College in Portland, Oregon, in 1951. After a semester of graduate study in linguistics at Indiana University, he returned west to attend graduate school at Berkeley in the department of East Asian languages. In the Bay Area, Snyder associated with Kenneth Rexroth, Robert Duncan, Philip Whalen, Allen Ginsberg, Jack Kerouac, and others who were part of the remarkable flowering of West Coast poetry during the fifties. In 1956 he moved to Kyoto, Japan, to study Zen Buddhism and East Asian culture. During his Japan years he traveled six months through India and Nepal, visiting ashrams, shrines, and temples, together with Allen Ginsberg and Joanne Kyger. In 1969 he returned to North America. For the last thirty-five years he has been living in the northern Sierra Nevada. He is married to Carole Koda, and has two sons and two stepdaughters. From 1986 until 2002, he taught part-time at the University of California at Davis, in the creative writing and the "Nature and Culture" programs. He has eighteen books of poetry and prose in print. *Turtle Island* (New Directions, 1974) won the Pulitzer Prize for Poetry in 1975, and his book-length poem *Mountains and Rivers Without End* (Counterpoint, 1996) won the Bollingen Prize. His most recent prose book is *The High Sierra of California* (Heyday Press, 2002), in collaboration with print artist Tom Killion.

Of "Waiting for a Ride," Snyder writes: "In 3500 B.C., the pole star was Thuban, in Draco. I'm very grateful that I had a few moments to reflect on my life while standing in the Austin, Texas, airport."

MAURA STANTON was born in Evanston, Illinois, in 1946. She received her BA from the University of Minnesota and her MFA from the University of Iowa. Her first book of poetry, *Snow on Snow*, won the Yale Series of Younger Poets Award. Her most recent collection of poetry, *Glacier Wine*, was published by Carnegie-Mellon University Press in 2001. *Cities in the Sea*, a collection of short stories, won the Michigan Literary Award and was published by the University of Michigan Press in 2003. She divides her time between Minneapolis and Bloomington, Indiana, where she teaches in the creative writing program at Indiana University.

Of "Twenty Questions," Stanton writes: "What came first, the question or the sonnet? My parents were married at the Madeleine in Paris, France, on July 17, 1945. Then they sailed home to America and raised nine children. The man next door to us in Minneapolis was a chemist who worked at General Mills. One day he brought over some fake bacon bits. They tasted great. Is that when I became a vegetarian? I always say yes to champagne. Charlie Chaplin's corpse was dug up and held for ransom—but nobody would pay it! The body snatchers were caught. I come from a happy family that loves to play games, so wasn't it inevitable that I'd try to combine that pleasure with the pleasure of writing a poem?"

DOROTHEA TANNING was born in Galesburg, Illinois, in 1910. She is an artist and writer whose paintings and sculpture are in major museum collections including the Tate Gallery, in London; the Centre Pompidou and the Musée de la Ville de Paris, both in Paris; the Philadelphia Museum of Art; the Menil Collection, in Houston; and the Chicago Art Institute. Besides poetry, her writing includes a memoir, *Between Lives* (W. W. Norton, 2001; pbk. Northwestern University Press, 2004), and a novel, *Chasm* (Overlook Press, 2004). Her first collection of poems, *A Table of Content*, was published in 2004 by Graywolf Press. She lives in New York City.

Of "End of the Day on Second," Tanning writes: "This poem is mostly about touch. And about its power, its solace, even. From the awesome to the humble, examples abound: God touches Adam's finger in Michelangelo's fresco; Jesus, resurrected, invites his friend to touch his wound. And people everywhere touch what they can—anything to prove they live, they choose, they are not alone. A city department store does wonders for this need."

JAMES TATE was born in Kansas City, Missouri, in 1943. His most recent book, *Return to the City of White Donkeys*, was published by Ecco/Harper-Collins in 2004. Among his other books are *Memoir of the Hawk* (Ecco, 2001), *Shroud of the Gnome* (Ecco, 1997); *Worshipful Company of Fletchers* (Ecco, 1994), winner of the National Book Award; and *Selected Poems* (Wesleyan University Press, 1991), which received the Pulitzer Prize. *The Route as Briefed* appeared in the University of Michigan Press's Poets on Poetry Series in 1999. He teaches at the University of Massachusetts in Amherst and was the guest editor of *The Best American Poetry 1997*.

Of "The Swing," James Tate writes: "President Clinton said he liked this poem because it reminded him of his childhood. As usual, I had no idea what he meant."

CHASE TWICHELL was born in New Haven, Connecticut, in 1950. She is the author of five books of poetry, most recently, *The Ghost of Eden* (1995) and *The Snow Watcher* (1998), both from Ontario Review Press. A new collection, *Dog Language*, is forthcoming from Copper Canyon. She translated, in collaboration with Tony K. Stewart, a sequence of poems by Rabindranath Tagore, *The Lover of God* (Copper Canyon, 2003). She is coeditor (with Robin Behn) of *The Practice of Poetry: Writing Exercises from Poets Who Teach* (HarperCollins, 1994). In 1999 she quit teaching (at Princeton University) to start Ausable Press, an independent literary press that publishes poetry. She lives with her husband, the novelist Russell Banks, in upstate New York.

Of "Marijuana," Twichell writes: "This poem revisits a rough but numinous year of adolescence which seems in retrospect to have been a major fulcrum in my life. Though most of the details are invented or composites of various times and places (the real ones long ago hijacked by memory the liar), the emotional gist seems to have survived intact, and that was what I wanted to investigate. I can't get closer to it than I did in the poem, but it's something akin to a weight born of the sense that anything was possible, both good and bad, that nothing had yet been chosen or closed off, determined. I can hardly imagine that mind now, yet every decision I make, every impulse or hesitation, has its roots in that same wilderness. As a Buddhist, I might say that the poem was an attempt to understand the notion of karma, the rippling of cause and effect through consciousness. As an ex-fisherman I might say it was a form of catch-and-release, an attempt to make contact if only for a moment with a kind of consciousness lost to me now."

DAVID WAGONER was born in Massillon, Ohio, in 1926. He has published seventeen books of poems, most recently, *Good Morning and Good Night* (University of Illinois Press, 2005), and ten novels, one of which, *The Escape Artist*, was made into a movie by Francis Ford Coppola in 1982. He won the Ruth Lilly Poetry Prize in 1991. He has taught at the University of Washington since 1954 and was the editor of *Poetry Northwest* until its demise in 2002.

Of "For a Man Who Wrote *CUNT* on a Motel Bathroom Mirror," Wagoner writes: "I found the word on the mirror when I checked in to a motel in Columbia, South Carolina, during a reading tour. I speculated then, as I did in the poem, about the circumstances, including the fact that the maid, who had just cleaned everything else in the room and bathroom, had skipped the mirror and had left it for me to mull over."

ROSANNA WARREN was born in Fairfield, Connecticut, in 1953. She worked for years at painting and drawing, and currently teaches comparative literature at Boston University, with an emphasis on literary translation and nineteenth- and twentieth-century French poetry. Her books of poems are *Departure* (W. W. Norton, 2003), *Stained Glass* (W. W. Norton, 1993), *Each Leaf Shines Separate* (W. W. Norton, 1984), and *Snow Day* (Palaemon Press, 1981). Her verse translation, with Stephen Scully, of Euripides' play *Suppliant Women* was published by Oxford University Press in 1995.

Warren writes: "'From the Notebooks of Anne Verveine, VII' is the most recent poem I have found/translated/composed from the note-books of the imaginary French poet Anne Verveine left in her *chambre de bonne* in Paris in January 2000, when she traveled to Uzbekistan. Verveine was born in 1965 in a village near Grasse, in the South of France, and after graduating from the *lycée* she lived obscurely in Paris, where she worked as a graphic designer for a small publisher of art books. She was last seen hitchhiking west of Bukhara, near the border of Turkmenistan, in August 2000. She is presumed kidnapped or dead.

"I needed Anne Verveine in order to write the erotic pastoral I couldn't compose under my own name. My American persona—too ironic, critical, and ethically convoluted—would not have allowed these poems. But history and politics always haunt the edges of pastoral, and the Silk Road and Uzbekistan are tough and tormented places. Pastoral exists only in the imagination, and in the traces it leaves on the page. (That is why Anne Verveine had to disappear)."

MARLYS WEST was born in Louisiana in 1966. She received her MFA in poetry from the Michener Center for Writers and held the Hodder Fellowship at Princeton University. *Notes for a Late-Blooming Martyr*, her book of poems, was published by the University of Akron Press in 1999. She works as a nonprofit consultant, mentor, and volunteer.

Of "Ballad of the Subcontractor," West writes: "I'd been reading about skyscraper construction, which set the scene for the subcontractor's soliloquy overlooking the Manhattan skyline. Originally I'd wanted more details about an actual construction site, but as the subcontractor sounded this lament his interior world felt more interesting so I took out the stanzas on safety nets and self-lifting cranes in order to keep the focus on Francis, his high-school nemesis."

SUSAN WHEELER was born in Pittsburgh, Pennsylvania, in 1955. She teaches in the creative writing programs of Princeton University and the New School in New York. She is the author of four collections of poetry, *Bag o' Diamonds* (University of Georgia Press, 1993), *Smokes* (Four Way Books, 1998), *Source Codes* (Salt Publishing, 2001), and *Ledger* (University of Iowa Press, 2005). Her novel, *Record Palace*, was published by Graywolf Press in 2005.

Of the anthologized excerpt from "The Maud Project," Wheeler writes: "My mother grew up in Topeka, Kansas, during the Great Depression. Grace Louise was the daughter of Olive Diffenderfer Skeen, who ran a boardinghouse after her husband left her; and the niece of Meldrum Clifton Diffenderfer, who ran a funeral home. These are four in a series of poems employing phrases my mother commonly used while I was growing up, and so make for a kind of autobiographical enterprise."

RICHARD WILBUR was born in New York City in 1921. He attended Amherst College and served, during World War II, with the Thirty-sixth Infantry Division. He retired from academic life in 1986, having taught at Harvard, Wellesley, Wesleyan, and Smith. He continues to play tennis and raise vegetables. His latest book, *Collected Poems 1943–2004* (Harcourt, 2004), contains all of his poems to date, a few lyrics from Broadway shows, and five books of verses and drawings for children and amusable adults. With his wife, Charlotte, he lives in Cummington, Massachusetts.

Of "Some Words Inside of Words," Wilbur writes: "My poems for children are mostly about connections, oppositions, and differences, and what they do is playfully to outrage the sense of order. Children know that the emperor has no clothes, and that the adult sense of reality is shaky. They enjoy a bit of chaos and a more limber patterning of the world. So do adults, in their better and braver moments."

CECILIA WOLOCH was born in Pittsburgh, Pennsylvania, in 1956, and grew up there and in rural Kentucky, one of seven children of a seamstress and an airplane mechanic. She attended Transylvania University in Lexington, Kentucky, earning degrees in English and theater arts, before moving to Los Angeles in 1979. She completed her MFA in creative writing at Antioch University in 1999. She has conducted poetry workshops for children and young people, participants in Elderhostel programs, and inmates at a prison for the criminally insane. She has taught at the University of Redlands, the University of Southern California, California State University at Northridge, the New England College MFA program in poetry, and Emory University in Atlanta. She is the founding director of Summer Poetry in Idyllwild and of the Paris Poetry Workshop. Her books of poems are *Sacrifice* (Cahuenga Press, 1997), *Tsigan: The Gypsy Poem* (Cahuenga Press, 2002) and *Late* (BOA Editions, Ltd., 2003). She spends part of each year on the road in the United States and Europe, and maintains residences in both Atlanta and Los Angeles.

Of "Bareback Pantoum," Woloch writes: "This poem began as a catalog of images from a memory of one night in the heat of my adolescence, in rural Kentucky. Someone had started a fire in the woods near our house, probably to burn some brush or scrap lumber from a house that was being built nearby, and the fire started to spread. Since the fire department wouldn't come out unless or until a structure had caught fire, my sister and I and two local boys—Boo and Tony were their names—decided to take it upon ourselves to keep watch through the night. Boo and Tony had borrowed some horses from another neighbor, but we didn't have saddles. Really, it was just an excuse for my sister and me to ride bareback behind those boys through the woods, holding on to their waists, and my mother knew it. She and my father kept watch from the house, I'm sure, but let us stay out there until nearly dawn. My mother had to write a note to excuse my absence from school the next day, and wrote a melodramatic and hilarious account of the whole episode, which I wish I'd saved; it's probably better and more accurate than the poem.

"When I started to write the poem, thirty-some years after the event, I wanted to capture the heart-galloping excitement I'd felt that night, the first stirrings of sexual drama; I wanted to try to write my own version of 'The Highwayman,' which I've loved since I was a girl and was first seduced by its dark rhythms. When the poem wasn't moving forward as a catalog, I decided to try taking the most rhythmic lines and shaping a pantoum from those. The poem seemed to come together pretty easily after that; the pattern of repetition seemed to fit perfectly my memory of riding back and forth between the woods and our house, and was deeply pleasurable, too. It was the first pantoum I'd ever written, and I felt as if I'd discovered a slightly wicked, lovely secret."

CHARLES WRIGHT was born in Pickwick Dam, Tennessee, in 1935, and was educated at Davidson College and the University of Iowa. His recent books, all from Farrar, Straus and Giroux, include *Buffalo Yoga* (2004), *A Short History of the Shadow* (2004), *Negative Blue: Selected Later Poems* (2000), and *Appalachia* (1998). *Black Zodiac* (1997) received a Pulitzer Prize and *Chickamauga* (1995) received the Lenore Marshall Prize. A new collection of poems, *Scar Tissue*, is forthcoming. Wright teaches at the University of Virginia in Charlottesville.

Of "A Short History of My Life," Wright writes: "My life is an open book, and here it is."

MATTHEW YEAGER was born in Cincinnati, Ohio, in 1979. At present, he writes poems, starts and abandons plays, and works as a delivery truck driver and caterer. He lives in New York City.

Of "A Big Ball of Foil in a Small New York Apartment," Yeager writes: "The poem is the growth of a small ball of foil into the largest ball of foil an apartment can hold. It is also the progression of the four similies (*egg* to *island* to *heart* to *world*) that lend their accompanying little or big realities to help the ball out. The poem is made out of scraps of foil a fellow has found and brought back. It plays by the rules of the physical world. The words that sing the ball into being (which I don't much care for anymore because they're too in the guy's head) are more or less just packaging. They are separate; I mean, after you read them you can separate them, tear them off like cellophane or a cardboard box, and the ball will still be there. Stylistically it is an oral poem. I think it is most enjoyable when sounded aloud, at a good clip, pausing at the ends of the lines. Then you get the momentum.

"Originally the foil ball was a simile in a sonnet from a sonnet series I have called the 'Gut Sonnets.' The Gut, a mean, detached belly from Indiana that secretly pens sonnets, described itself as feeling 'useless as a big ball of foil' after having been fed and fed to help a fraternity of nerds win a tug-of-war competition. Imagining the big foil ball pleased me and I decided to give it a canvas to itself. Foil is very beautiful. Living here, you see a lot of it just walking around, bright-shining out from among the other blown-around trash. As an object, a foil ball is unique. When alone, it will reject perspective. It needs to be put into perspective, set next to something of definite size. Another thing that makes it unique is that in growing it does not change, but simply becomes more of what it is.

"As for the writing, the thing was to make the ball of foil into a ball of foil. Because the context is poetry and a big foil ball is absurd, there's an inclination to try to interpret it into something else. But it is just a big ball of foil. This isn't to say the ball refuses the metaphorical. That's the fun, actually. But rinsing or twisting the language to make the ball seem a stand-in for something that can accrete and take over a life (love, art, sneakers, a big secret, whatever) would have limited the ball to a particular otherness.

"The poem of the ball also has to do with external limitation—and therefore with form. Form's boundaries both encourage and discourage. While the ceiling and walls may stop the ball builder's progress, I would argue that they spur him on by marking off possibility's realm. If our fellow happened to live in a cathedral, he wouldn't have tried to go all the way. The hugeness of the space would have been too daunting.

"There is actually a sequel to the poem. The epigraph is from one of my favorite poems, 'God's Grandeur' by Hopkins."

KEVIN YOUNG was born in Lincoln, Nebraska, in 1970, but moved to Boston before he was one year old; his family hails from Louisiana. He is the author of four books of poems, including *Black Maria* (Knopf, 2005) and *Jelly Roll* (Knopf, 2003). He is the editor of *Giant Steps: The New Generation of African American Writers* (HarperCollins, 2001), *Blues Poems* (Everyman Pocket Poets, 2003), and most recently, the Library of America's *John Berryman: Selected Poems* (2004). He is Atticus Haygood Professor of English and creative writing and curator of the Danowski Collection at Emory University.

Young writes: "'Black Cat Blues' first appeared as part of 'Watching the Good Trains Go By,' a suite of poems written to accompany photomontages by Romare Bearden. The poems also appeared with an introductory headnote that reads, in part: 'I have thought of this suite of poems less as a collaboration with Bearden than as inspired and confirmed by Bearden, almost in a religious sense—his aesthetic, so matched as it is to what used to be called Afro-American culture, seemed best honored by a range of blues and moods. He helps us all to see the ways in which the blues aesthetic—which rears its tragicomic head in Bearden in everything from cardplayers to a jumble of faces—is one of collage. Indeed, collage may be one way to understand the blues method: gathering the best floating lines from all over creation in order to make a blues of one's own. I wanted many of the poems here to sound like something hauntingly familiar, like something heard before, whether gossip or song. Or a collage, with its original elements intact but fractured into something new. After the blues of my last book (*Jelly Roll*) where the music provided a guide to the personal, I see the blues here more as trying to capture the historic sense of the blues—how to evoke history in just a title, or a phrase, or a sliver of a face.'"

MAGAZINES WHERE THE POEMS
WERE FIRST PUBLISHED

American Letters & Commentary, ed. Anna Rabinowitz; poetry ed. Matthea Harvey. 850 Park Ave., Ste 5B, New York, NY 10021.

American Poetry Review, eds. Stephen Berg, David Bonanno, and Arthur Vogelsang. 117 S. 17th St., Ste 910, Philadelphia, PA 19103.

The American Scholar, poetry ed. Rob Farnsworth (for 2004); Langdon Hammer (henceforth). 1606 New Hampshire Ave., NW, Washington, DC 20009.

The Antioch Review, poetry ed. Judith Hall. PO Box 148, Yellow Springs, OH 45387.

The Atlantic Monthly, poetry ed. Peter Davison (1928–2004). 77 N. Washington St., Boston, MA 02114.

Barrow Street, eds. Patricia Carlin, Peter Covino, Lois Hirshkowitz, and Melissa Hotchkiss. PO Box 1831, New York, NY 10156.

Beloit Poetry Journal, eds. John Rosenwald and Lee Sharkey. PO Box 151, Farmington, ME 04938.

BOMB, ed. Betsy Sussler, 80 Hanson Pl., Ste 703, Brooklyn, NY 11217.

Boston Review, poetry ed. Timothy Donnelly. E53-407 MIT, Cambridge, MA 02139.

The Cincinnati Review, poetry ed. James Cummins (for 2004); Don Bogen (henceforth). PO Box 210069, Cincinnati, OH 45221-0069.

Conduit, ed. William D. Waltz, 510 Eighth Ave. NE, Minneapolis, MN 55413.

Court Green, eds. Arielle Greenberg, Tony Trigilio, and David Trinidad. Columbia College Chicago, English Dept., 600 S. Michigan Ave., Chicago, IL 60605.

Crazyhorse, poetry eds. Carol Ann Davis and Garrett Doherty. Dept. of English, College of Charleston, 66 George St., Charleston, SC 29424.

CROWD, ed. Aimee Kelly; poetry ed. Brett Fletcher Lauer. 487 Union St. #3, Brooklyn, NY 11231.

Denver Quarterly, ed. Bin Ramke. 2000 E. Asbury, Denver, CO 80208.

88: A Journal of Contemporary American Poetry, managing ed. Ian Randall Wilson. c/o Hollyridge Press, PO Box 2872, Venice, CA 90294.

Epoch, ed. Michael Koch; ed. for vol. 52, no. 3 (2004) Roger Gilbert. 251 Goldwin Smith Hall, Ithaca, NY 14853-3201.

Fence, poetry eds. Matthew Rohrer, Christopher Stackhouse, and Max Winter. 303 E. Eighth St. #B1, New York, NY 10009.

Gastronomica, ed. Darra Goldstein. University of California Press Journals, 2000 Center St., Ste 303, Berkeley, CA 94704-1223.

Good Foot, eds. Amanda Lea Johnson, Katherine Sarkis, and Carmine G. Simmons. PO Box 681, Murray Hill Station, New York, NY 10156.

Gulf Coast, eds. Michael Dumanis, Miho Nonaka, and Todd Samuelson. English Dept., University of Houston, Houston, TX 77204-3013.

Hanging Loose, eds. Robert Hershon, Dick Lourie, Mark Pawlak, and Ron Schreiber (1934–2004). 231 Wyckoff St., Brooklyn, NY 11217.

The Hudson Review, ed. Paula Deitz. 684 Park Ave., New York, NY 10021.

Image, ed. Gregory Wolfe. 3307 Third Ave., West Seattle, WA 98119.

In Posse Review, poetry ed. Ilya Kaminsky. http://www.webdelsol.com/InPosse.

Insurance Magazine, eds. Kostas Anagnopoulos and Chris Tokar. 132 N. First St. #11, Brooklyn, NY 11211.

The Iowa Review, ed. David Hamilton. 308 EPB, University of Iowa, Iowa City, IA 52242.

Jacket, ed. John Tranter. http://www.jacketmagazine.com.

jubilat, eds. Christian Hawkey and Michael Teig. Dept. of English, 482 Bartlett Hall, University of Massachusetts, Amherst, MA 01003-0510.

LIT, ed. Justin Marks; poetry ed. J. Branson Housley. New School Writing Program, 66 W. 12th St., Rm 508, New York, NY 10011.

The Los Angeles Review, eds. Gail Wronsky and Mark Salerno. Red Hen Press, PO Box 3537, Granada Hills, CA 91394.

Michigan Quarterly Review, ed. Laurence Goldstein. 3574 Rackham Bldg., 915 E. Washington St., Ann Arbor, MI 48109-1070.

Mudfish, ed. Jill Hoffman. 184 Franklin St., New York, NY 10013.

New American Writing, eds. Maxine Chernoff and Paul Hoover. 369 Molino Ave., Mill Valley, CA 94941.

The New Criterion, poetry ed. Robert Richman (for 2004); David Yezzi (henceforth). 900 Broadway, Ste 602, New York, NY 10003.

New England Review, poetry ed. C. Dale Young. Middlebury College, Middlebury, VT 05753.

New Letters, ed. Robert Stewart, UMKC University House, 5101 Rockhill Rd., Kansas City, MO 64110-2499.

New York Quarterly, ed. Raymond Hammond; literary ed. Malachi Black. PO Box 693, Old Chelsea Station, New York, NY 10113.

The New Yorker, poetry ed. Alice Quinn. 4 Times Square, New York, NY 10036.

Notre Dame Review, poetry ed. John Matthias. 840 Flanner Hall, University of Notre Dame, Notre Dame, IN 46556.

Open City, eds. Thomas Beller and Joanna Yas. 270 Lafayette St., Ste 1412, New York, NY 10012.

The Paris Review, poetry ed. Richard Howard. 541 E. 72 St., New York, NY 10021.

Pleiades, poetry ed. Wayne Miller. Dept. of English, Central Missouri State University, Warrensburg, MO 64093.

Pleine Marge, publisher Jacqueline Chéniaux. 52, blvd Saint-Michel, F-75006 Paris, France.

Ploughshares, poetry ed. David Daniel. Emerson College, 120 Boylston St., Boston, MA 02116.

PN Review, ed. Michael Schmidt. 4th Fl., Alliance House, Cross St., Manchester M2 7AP, United Kingdom.

Poetry, ed. Christian Wiman. 1030 N. Clark St., Ste 420, Chicago, IL 60610.

Poetry Daily, eds. Rob Anderson, Diane Boller, Don Selby. http://www.poems.com.

POOL: A Journal of Poetry, eds. Amy Schroeder and Judith Taylor. PO Box 49738, Los Angeles, CA 90049

Runes: A Review of Poetry, eds. CB Follett and Susan Terris. c/o Arctos Press, PO Box 401, Sausalito, CA 94966.

Salt, ed. John Kinsella. PO Box 937, Great Wilbraham, Cambridge CB1 5JX, United Kingdom.

Sentence: a Journal of Prose Poetics, ed. Brian Clements. Box 7, Western Connecticut State University, 181 White St., Danbury, CT 06810.

Shankpainter, eds. Winter Fellows of Provincetown's Fine Arts Work Center. Provincetown, MA. http://www.fawc.org.

Shenandoah, ed. R. T. Smith. Mattingly House, 2 Lee Ave., Washington and Lee University, Lexington, VA 24450-0303.

Slate, poetry ed. Robert Pinsky. http://www.slate.com.

Sycamore Review, poetry eds. Sarah Green and Rebecca Bednarz. Purdue University, Dept. of English, 500 Oval Dr., West Lafayette, IN 47907-2038.

32 Poems, eds. John Poch and Deborah Ager. PO Box 5824, Hyattsville, MD 20782.

Verse, eds. Brian Henry and Andrew Zawacki. Department of English, University of Georgia, Athens, GA 30602.

Verse Daily, eds. Hunter Hamilton and Campbell Russo. http://www.versedaily.org.

Virginia Quarterly Review, ed. Ted Genoways; poetry chair David Lee Rubin. University of Virginia, One West Range, Box 400223, Charlottesville, VA 22904-4223.

The Yale Review, ed. J. D. McClatchy. Yale University, PO Box 208243, New Haven, CT 06520-8243.

ACKNOWLEDGMENTS

The series editor wishes to thank Mark Bibbins for his invaluable assistance. J. D. Bullard, Shanna Compton, James Cummins, Peter Davis, Denise Duhamel, Stacey Harwood, Susan Hutton, Deborah Landau, Kelly Nichols, Danielle Pafunda, Karl Parker, Liam Rector, and Michael Schiavo made useful suggestions or helped in other ways. Warm thanks go also to Glen Hartley, Lynn Chu, and Katy Sprinkel of Writers' Representatives, and to Alexis Gargagliano, Erica Gelbard, Erich Hobbing, and John McGhee of Scribner.

Grateful acknowledgment is made of the magazines in which these poems first appeared and the magazine editors who selected them. A sincere attempt has been made to locate all copyright holders. Unless otherwise noted, copyright to the poems is held by the individual poets.

A. R. Ammons: "In View of the Fact" appeared in *Epoch*. Reprinted by permission of the Estate of A. R. Ammons.

John Ashbery: "In Dearest, Deepest Winter" appeared in *Crazyhorse*. Reprinted by permission of the poet.

Maureen Bloomfield: "The Catholic Encyclopedia" appeared in *The Cincinnati Review*. Reprinted by permission of the poet.

Catherine Bowman: "I Want to Be Your Shoebox" appeared in *Open City*. Reprinted by permission of the poet.

Stephanie Brown: "Roommates: Noblesse Oblige, *Sprezzatura*, and Gin Lane" appeared in *POOL*. Reprinted by permission of the poet.

Charles Bukowski: "The Beats" appeared in *New York Quarterly*. Reprinted by permission of Ecco/HarperCollins.

Elena Karina Byrne: "Irregular Masks" appeared in *The Los Angeles Review*. Reprinted by permission of the poet.

Victoria Chang: "Seven Changs" appeared in *Michigan Quarterly Review*. Reprinted by permission of the poet.

Shanna Compton: "To Jacques Pépin" appeared in *Gastronomica*. Reprinted by permission of the poet.

James Cummins: "The Poets March on Washington" appeared in *Jacket*. Reprinted by permission of the poet.

Terrance Hayes: "Variations on Two Black Cinema Treasures" appeared in *CROWD*. Reprinted by permission of the poet.

Samuel Hazo: "Seesaws" from *A Flight to Elsewhere*. © 2005 by Samuel Hazo. Reprinted by permission of the poet and Autumn House Press. First appeared in *The Atlantic Monthly*.

Anthony Hecht: "Motes" appeared in *The New Yorker*. Reprinted by permission of the Estate of Anthony Hecht.

Jennifer Michael Hecht: "The Propagation of the Species" appeared in *In Posse Review*. Reprinted by permission of the poet.

Lyn Hejinian: from *The Fatalist* appeared in *The Fatalist*. © 2003 by Lyn Hejinian. Reprinted by permission of the poet and Omnidawn Publishing. First appeared in *BOMB*.

Ruth Herschberger: "Remorse After a Panic Attack in a Wisconsin Field, 1975" appeared in *New Letters*. Reprinted by permission of the poet.

Jane Hirshfield: "Burlap Sack" appeared in *Runes: A Review of Poetry*. Reprinted by permission of the poet.

Tony Hoagland: "In a Quiet Town by the Sea" appeared in *The Cincinnati Review*. Reprinted by permission of the poet.

Vicki Hudspith: "Ants" appeared in *Mudfish*. Reprinted by permission of the poet.

Donald Justice: "A Chapter in the Life of Mr. Kehoe, Fisherman" from *Collected Poems*. © The Literary Estate of Donald Justice. Reprinted by permission of Random House/Alfred A. Knopf and Co. First appeared in *The New Criterion*.

Mary Karr: "A Blessing from My Sixteen Years' Son" appeared in *The New Yorker*. Reprinted by permission of the poet.

Garret Keizer: "Hell and Love" appeared in *Image*. Reprinted by permission of the poet.

Brigit Pegeen Kelly: "The Wolf" from *The Orchard*. © 2004 by Brigit Pegeen Kelly. Reprinted by permission of BOA Editions, Ltd. First appeared in *32 Poems*.

Galway Kinnell: "Shelley" appeared in *The New Yorker*. Reprinted by permission of the poet.

Rachel Loden: "In the Graveyard of Fallen Monuments" first appeared in *Denver Quarterly* and *In the Graveyard of Fallen Monuments* (Wild Honey Press, Ireland, 2005). Reprinted by permission of the poet.

Sarah Manguso: "Hell" appeared in *Conduit*. Reprinted by permission of the poet.

Printed in the United States
By Bookmasters